ROCK
MINERALS

A GUIDE TO FAMILIAR MINERALS, GEMS, ORES AND ROCKS

By
HERBERT S. ZIM, Ph.D.

and
PAUL R. SHAFFER, Ph.D.

Illustrated by
RAYMOND PERLMAN

A LITTLE GUIDE IN COLOUR

PAUL HAMLYN

London / New York / Sydney / Toronto

CONTENTS

GOLD CRYSTAL

Published by The Hamlyn Publishing Group Ltd
Hamlyn House, Feltham, Middlesex, England
by arrangement with Golden Press, Inc.
© Copyright 1957 Golden Press, Inc.
First English Edition 1965
Eighth reprint 1973
ISBN 0 601 07985 X
Printed in Italy by Arnoldo Mondadori Editore - Verona

| flint knife | bronze knife | iron knife (bronze handle) |
| 14,000 B.C. | 500 B.C. | A.D. 200 |

ROCKS AND MAN

Man first used rock when he began taking shelter in caves. At the same time, he used stones as weapons, both against his enemies and against the animals he preyed on. This was the Stone Age. In it, not only was man housed in stone, but all his weapons and tools were of stone. We are proud of the progress we have made since then, and, indeed, in the course of a million years we have enormously increased our technical prowess, yet our basic materials are still derived from the same source. Modern arms, including atomic bombs, like our houses – even those made of glass or aluminium – have originated from rocks. It is impossible to imagine that it will ever be otherwise. The further we advance, the longer becomes the list of the products extracted from the earth. Every part of an aeroplane and the petrol it consumes, all kitchen material from plates to refrigerators and including the gas we cook on, are derived from the earth's crust. There is not a single industry which does not depend, directly or indirectly, on rocks.

What are rocks? They are a combination of minerals which, in turn, are chemical substances, almost all crystalline, built up of atoms of a relatively small number of elements. But our knowledge of rocks is, in fact, still confined to those which have cooled down to form a solid coating all round the world called the earth's crust. The continents of the world are islands, composed of the lighter rocks floating on the inner mass of heavier rocks, far down beyond our reach, and still at very high temperatures.

The hundred-odd elements of which all the matter in our universe is composed are all found in our world, though in greatly varying quantities. The most common is oxygen, believed to form 53% by weight of the earth's substance, the next being silicon, 26%. There follow: aluminium, 7.45%; iron, 4.2%; calcium, 3.3%; potassium, 3%; hydrogen, 1%; carbon, 0.4%; etc. The various combinations of these elements form about 1500 different minerals.

A given rock may be formed of one or several minerals, and its properties will depend on its components. Though most are hard, some are not; they may be plastic, like clay, powdery, like sand, or even liquid, like petroleum.

The study of the earth's crust and its composition has developed to such an extent in recent times that

mountains

lava

continental mass of granite

ocean

island

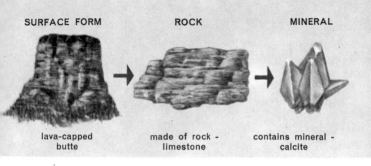

SURFACE FORM	ROCK	MINERAL
lava-capped butte	made of rock - limestone	contains mineral - calcite

it is now undertaken by a number of sciences, each with its own specialists. To *geologists* fall the tasks of identifying and surveying the rock formations of the earth and determining how and when they were formed, to *petrologists* that of identifying and classifying the rocks themselves, and to *mineralogists* that of identifying and studying the minerals of which the rocks are composed. Other specialists concentrate on the study of coal and other fuels on which our industry depends, and the principles to be observed when prospecting for them.

These important branches of knowledge have only developed in modern times. A hundred years ago the first oil prospectors in America threw their hats in the air and started drilling wherever they happened to fall. We may smile today at their primitive methods, but they had already made great progress compared to the Russian scientists who, fifty years earlier, had declared petroleum to be a useless product.

The map on the two following pages shows us the principal mines and oil-fields at present being worked in Europe. They represent only a small portion of the

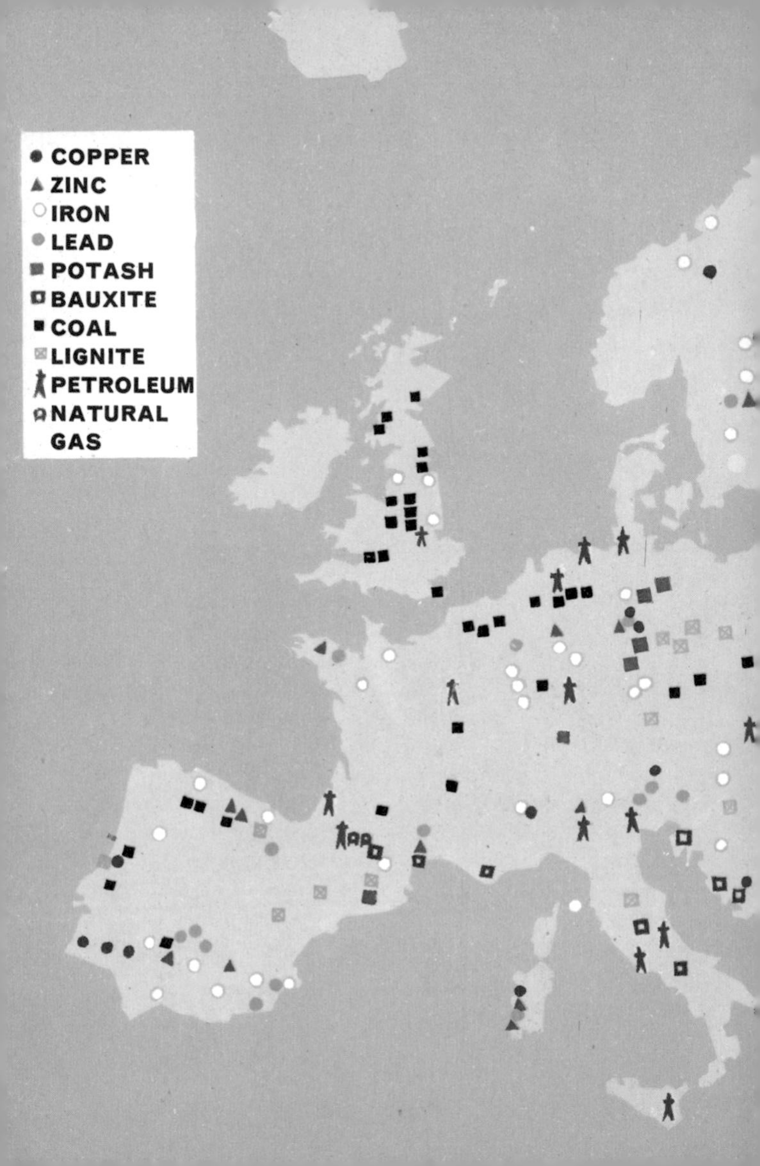

- ● COPPER
- ▲ ZINC
- ○ IRON
- ● LEAD
- ▰ POTASH
- ▱ BAUXITE
- ■ COAL
- ▦ LIGNITE
- ⚚ PETROLEUM
- ⌂ NATURAL GAS

wealth that is being produced from the earth. If we were to add the materials used for building, the rare earths, fertilizers, valuable and precious stones, etc., the map would be so crowded as to be unintelligible. The bulk of the land of Europe is devoted to agriculture, however, and here again it is more or less directly to rocks that we are indebted for the production of all our foodstuffs. Without arable land there would be no crops, without crops there would be no animals and no men either.

But all this wealth, derived from the earth, is not inexhaustible. Most of the earth's products could eventually be reconstituted, but it would take millions of times as long as we have taken to use and often, in fact, to waste them.

Soil, like petrol and uranium, is practically irreplaceable. So, for that matter, are the mineral specimens you may collect. Think of that when you make an interesting discovery, think of the other people that may come after you.

A limestone quarry

Riker mount

Mineral cabinet

COLLECTING FOR AMATEURS

Collecting specimens of rocks and minerals is the first step towards a knowledge of the subject. Moreover, it provides physical exercise in the open air; it keeps the mind occupied by constant observation, without imposing the long spells of immobility required of animal watchers; lastly it is an activity that, unlike the botanist's, may be pursued at all times, regardless of the season.

Where can it be carried out? Anywhere where rocks have been laid bare by natural forces – river banks, cliffs, etc. – but also where they have been uncovered artificially. It is indeed in these places – railway cuttings, quarries, tunnels and excavations in the neighbourhood of mines, etc. – that you may make your best finds, particularly if the work has recently been carried out. Never fail to ask permission to collect specimens, since the removal of a piece of rock may cause a landslide.

At the same time learn, as you walk about, to read the past history of the landscape before you. The rocks themselves and the geological formations may have much to tell you, and so may the vegetation. Gradually you will learn to plan your explorations in advance. Always ask advice from those who know more than you do, and try to visit any collection of minerals there may be in the local museum.

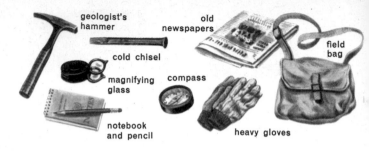

geologist's hammer

old newspapers

field bag

cold chisel

magnifying glass

compass

notebook and pencil

heavy gloves

YOUR EQUIPMENT should be kept to the minimum. First of all you need some old newspaper in which to wrap up your specimens, and a notebook in which to write notes on what you find. Generally, you will have to break away a piece of rock, and for this you need a geologist's hammer (get one of good quality) and a cold chisel. A magnifying glass, a compass, a pair of thick gloves and a knife are also useful. Do not take too much. A bag of specimens is heavy enough.

YOUR SPECIMENS should be chosen with care. Make sure they have been broken off recently. Choose those that are the size of your fist, unless you possess a little microscope; in that case they need be no bigger than a thimble.

It is often useful to bring home more than one specimen of the same rock. They may at first sight have seemed exactly alike but, on closer examination, show interesting differences. Don't take too many however; two or three should suffice. Your choice made, wrap up your specimens and label them with the date and the position in which they were found.

THE MAKING OF A REAL COLLECTION is quite another matter. The keeping of your specimens requires a good deal of space and, unless you have cabinets with well-fitting drawers, you will have a lot of trouble with dust.

IDENTIFICATION of your specimens can be done with the help of this book, and the next chapter is devoted to the various methods employed. But you must not expect to be able to identify immediately all the specimens you find. When in doubt, compare them with those in a museum.

CLASSIFICATION will depend on the purpose for which your collection is formed. The classification employed in this handbook is very simple; but whichever you choose, the classification will facilitate the identification and comparison of minerals, thus forming a sound basis for the study of the subject.

THE ARRANGEMENT of the collection begins with the numbering of each specimen in Indian ink on a small patch of quick-drying enamel paint. This number

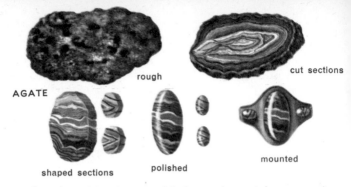

rough

cut sections

AGATE

shaped sections

polished

mounted

refers to entries in a card index and a catalogue, each of which will include the date and place of origin, the name of the rock or mineral, and, in the catalogue, any other particulars you think fit to note. The card index and catalogue will become more and more useful in helping you to identify fresh specimens.

The aims of amateur mineralogists are various. Some concentrate on semi-precious stones, or those remarkable in other ways; fossils, incrustations, etc. Others specialize in rock photography or stone-carving. Some are interested in a particular physical property, such as luminescence or radio-activity. Those interested in chemistry, on the other hand, will find abundant scope for that science in their collection.

The real 'addicts', however, are those who give themselves purely to the observation and study of rocks and minerals. They start by collecting as many specimens as possible. Eventually they will have the choice of various ways of specializing. They may concentrate on the minerals of their locality, for instance, or they may concentrate on minerals of a particular sort. Without going that far, however, who can deny the pleasure to be derived from recognizing the various rocks met with in the course of a walk?

JADEITE is sodium aluminium silicate ($NaAlSi_2O_6$). Colour: white, yellow, brown, or green. Often a gem (p. 88); seldom as crystals.

SPODUMENE is lithium aluminium silicate ($LiAlSi_2O_6$); opaque-white, lilac, or yellow. Rarely a transparent crystalline gem stone.

IDENTIFYING MINERALS

MINERALS ARE CHEMICALS They are chemical elements or compounds found naturally in the crust of the earth. They are inorganic, in contrast to organic chemicals (made mainly of carbon, hydrogen, and oxygen) typical of living things. Some minerals have a fixed chemical composition. Others are a series of related compounds in which one metallic element may wholly or partly replace another. The two minerals above are very similar chemically and in some of their physical properties, but are usually quite different in colour and other physical properties. Only rarely will a single physical or chemical property identify a mineral. Usually more characteristics must be used. These physical and chemical properties are described on pp. 14 to 24. Some are inherent and reliable; others are variable and must be used with care. You can easily learn to use the simpler physical and chemical tests. Identification of many rare minerals often requires expensive laboratory equipment and detailed chemical and optical tests which only an expert can make.

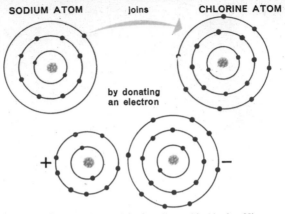

SODIUM ATOM   joins   CHLORINE ATOM

by donating
an electron

to form ionic crystal of sodium chloride (p. 68)

ELEMENTS are the building blocks of all materials, including minerals and rocks. About 100 elements are known. A dozen or so were known in ancient times; the latest were found in atom-splitting experiments. All are made up of protons, neutrons, and electrons. These, combined, form atoms of matter. The atoms in turn join to form molecules—the smallest particles usually produced in chemical reactions. When temperatures are high, molecules may break down into atoms or atom groups. With slow cooling these may join together, in regular order, to form crystals. Most minerals are crystalline, being formed from cooling mixtures, liquids, or vapours in the crust of the earth.

The arrangement of an atom's electrons determines with what other elements it will combine, and in what proportions. The physical conditions in molten materials also set the pattern by which chemical elements form different minerals. The science of physical chemistry has much to reveal about how, why, and when minerals form.

INTERFERENCE PATTERNS are shown by this thin section of a rock rich in pyroxene, here viewed through a polarizing microscope.

BIAXIAL INTERFERENCE FIGURE forms when a thin sheet of muscovite mica is examined through a polarizing microscope.

OPTICAL PROPERTIES of minerals are used mainly by experts, but amateurs should know about them because they are fundamental in precise mineral identification. Optical identification is highly accurate and can be used with particles of microscopic size. Pieces of minerals or rocks are mounted on slides, then ground till paper thin. These thin sections are examined through ordinary and polarized light. The bending of light as it passes through the minerals gives patterns that aid in identification. X-rays sent through thin fragments or powders produce a pattern dependent on the structure of the molecules and so are an aid to identification. Fragments of minerals can be immersed in transparent liquids of different density to measure their index of refraction. This is distinct for each mineral and is related to its crystal system (pp. 16-17). Thus an expert can tell if a diamond or emerald is real or false without doing any damage to the stone. It is worth paying more attention to these optical properties as you become more experienced.

A check on this diamond's index of refraction shows that bottom is cemented glass.

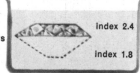

index 2.4

index 1.8

CRYSTAL FORM is critical in mineral identification as it reflects the structure of the very molecules of the mineral. It is also the most difficult characteristic to use and one that requires the most careful study. Yet crystals are so magnificent in their beauty and symmetry it is sometimes hard to believe they are natural. The study of how they are formed reveals mathematical relationships as amazing and as beautiful as the crystals

GALENA   HALITE

Cubic (Isometric) System includes crystals in which the three axes (common to five of six systems) are of equal length and are at right angles to one another, as in a cube—examples: galena, garnet, pyrite, and halite.

ZIRCON   RUTILE

Tetragonal System has two axes of equal length and one unequal. All three axes are at right angles to one another, as in zircon, rutile, and cassiterite.

QUARTZ   CALCITE

Hexagonal System has three equal axes at 120° angles arranged in one plane and one more axis of a different length at right angles to these, as in quartz, beryl, calcite, tourmaline, and cinnabar.

themselves. Perfect crystals are rare, and some are of great value. However, a fragment or an imperfect crystal will yield basic data to the experienced mineralogist. Sometimes crystals develop in clusters, or as twins. They reveal distortions, inclusions, and other interruptions in their development. A very simple outline of the six systems of crystals is given on these two pages as a bare introduction to the science of crystallography:

Orthorhombic System has crystals with three axes all at right angles, but all of different length. Examples: sulphur, barite, celestite, staurolite, and olivine.

SULPHUR   STAUROLITE

Monoclinic System has three unequal axes, two of which are not at right angles. The third makes a right angle to the plane of the other two, as in orthoclase, gypsum, micas, augite, epidote, and hornblende.

EPIDOTE   AUGITE

Triclinic System has three unequal axes but none forms a right angle with any other. Examples: plagioclase feldspars, rhodonite, and chalcanthite.

AMAZONSTONE   RHODONITE

A scratches B

B does not
scratch A

Try to scratch
A with B

Try to scratch
B with A

HARDNESS is used in a rough manner in mineral identification. There are much more precise ways of measuring hardness in industrial laboratories. Though arbitrary, Mohs' scale of ten minerals is useful:

1. Talc
2. Gypsum
3. Calcite
4. Fluorite
5. Apatite
6. Orthoclase
7. Quartz
8. Topaz
9. Corundum
10. Diamond

Remember these ten by using the odd sentence "The Girls Can Flirt And Other Queer Things Can Do". Gypsum is harder than talc but not twice as hard; fluorite is harder than calcite and less hard than apatite. If an unknown will scratch all the minerals in the scale up to 4 and is scratched by apatite, its hardness is between 4 and 5. Check carefully to be sure there is a distinct scratch. Don't test hardness on the face of a valuable crystal. For field use here are some other convenient standards of hardness:

fingernail
2.5

halfpenny
4

knife
blade
5.5

window
glass
5.5

steel
file
6.5

A balance used to measure specific gravity

SPECIFIC GRAVITY is the relative weight of a mineral compared to the weight of an equal volume of water. Since the weight of an equal volume of water is identical with the mineral's loss in weight when weighed in water, specific gravity (Sp. Gr.) is quickly determined. A corundum crystal weighing 2.0 oz. dry weighs 1.5 oz. when suspended in water. The loss (0.5 oz.) divided into the dry weight gives a specific gravity of 4.0. This may seem odd, because corundum contains only aluminium (Sp. Gr. 2.5) and oxygen, a gas. Learn to estimate specific gravity and make your own measurements as an aid to identification. Below are some average figures.

Borax	1.7	Talc	2.8	Corundum	4.0
Sulphur	2.0	Muscovite	2.8	Rutile	4.2
Halite	2.1	Tremolite	3.0	Barite	4.5
Stibnite	2.2	Apatite	3.2	Zircon	4.7
Gypsum	2.3	Crocidolite	3.3	Zincite	5.5
Serpentine	2.5	Topaz	3.5	Cassiterite	7.0
Orthoclase	2.6	Rhodochrosite	3.6	Cinnabar	8.0
Quartz	2.7	Staurolite	3.7	Uraninite	9.5
Calcite	2.7	Siderite	3.9	Gold	19.3

(Sp. Gr. of some minerals may vary as much as 25 per cent from specimen to specimen.)

aluminium
Sp. Gr. 2.5

+

oxygen
a gas

=

corundum
Sp. Gr. 4.0

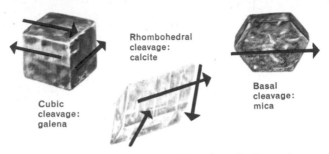

Cubic
cleavage:
galena

Rhombohedral
cleavage:
calcite

Basal
cleavage:
mica

CLEAVAGE is the way some minerals split along planes related to the molecular structure of the mineral and parallel to possible crystal faces. The perfection of cleavage is described in five steps from poor (as in bornite) to fair, good, perfect, and eminent (as in micas). The types of cleavage are usually described by the number and direction of cleavage planes. Three examples of cleavage are shown above. Use cleavage as an aid in identification—though you may at first find it difficult to tell the face of a crystal from a fresh, perfect cleavage surface.

Fracture is the breakage of a mineral specimen in some way other than along cleavage planes. Not all minerals show good cleavage; most show fracture. Fresh fractures show the mineral's true colour. Five to seven types of fracture are recognized; three are shown below.

Conchoidal
fracture:
obsidian

Uneven
fracture:
arsenopyrite

Earthy
fracture:
clay

COLOUR is the first of three characteristics that have to do with the way a mineral looks. In most metallic ores it is a safe clue in identification. But in quartz, corundum, calcite, fluorite, agate, garnet, tourmaline, and others it is often due to impurities and may vary greatly. So use colour with caution and use only the colour of a freshly broken surface. Note the surface tarnish on some metallic ores; it differs from the true colour, but can be used for identification also.

TOURMALINE CRYSTAL

CORUNDUM

Streak is the colour of the powdered mineral best seen when the mineral is rubbed against a streak plate of unglazed porcelain (the back of a tile is excellent). In metallic ores the streak may differ from the colour and so is worth noting.

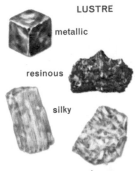

USING A STREAK PLATE

Lustre depends on the absorption, reflection, or refraction of light by the surface of a mineral. It is often an aid in identification. About a dozen terms are used, most of which are self-explanatory: *adamantine* (brilliant), like diamond; *vitreous* (glassy), like quartz; and *metallic* (like metal), like galena. The prefix *sub-* is used when the characteristic is less clear. Other lustres to note: dull, earthy, silky, greasy, pearly, resinous.

LUSTRE

metallic

resinous

silky

glassy

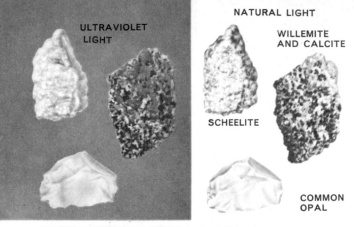

ULTRAVIOLET LIGHT

NATURAL LIGHT

WILLEMITE AND CALCITE

SCHEELITE

COMMON OPAL

ULTRAVIOLET LIGHT is invisible. Its waves are too short to be detected by the eye. However, some minerals, when exposed to this light, are "excited"—they absorb the ultraviolet light and emit longer light rays which we see as colours. Minerals which do this are *fluorescent*. If they continue to emit light after the ultraviolet rays have been cut off, they are *phosphorescent* (like the luminous dial of a watch). A quartz lamp is a fine source of ultraviolet light of short (about 1/10,000 in.) wavelength. An argon light gives longer ultraviolet rays. Not all minerals fluoresce when exposed to ultraviolet light. Uranium minerals do; so does scheelite, an ore of tungsten, and other tungsten minerals. Other minerals may fluoresce because of impurities, and still others fluoresce when from one locality and not when from another; this makes the search for fluorescent minerals exciting. A portable quartz lamp can be used on field trips. Because of their beauty, fluorescent minerals receive a good deal of attention, but the serious study of fluorescence is a difficult one.

MAGNETISM occurs in a few minerals. Lodestone (a form of magnetite) is a natural magnet. A magnet will attract bits of magnetite and pyrrhotite. A few manganese, nickel, and iron-titanium ores become magnetic when heated by a blowpipe.

Pyrrhotite is magnetic

ELECTRICAL PROPERTIES of minerals are varied. Thin slabs of quartz crystal control radio frequencies. Crystals of sulphur, topaz, and other minerals develop an electric charge when rubbed. Tourmaline crystals, when heated, develop opposite charges at opposite ends of the crystal.

Heated tourmaline develops electric charges

HEAT may raise the temperature of a mineral till it will fuse in a blowpipe flame. Use only small, thin splinters. The seven-point scale of fusibility, with examples, is:

1. **Stibnite** fuses in spirit lamp or candle flame (980°F)
2. **Chalcopyrite** fuses easily in blow-pipe flame (1475°F)
3. **Almandite** fuses less easily in blowpipe flame (1920°F)
4. **Actinolite:** thin edges fuse easily with blowpipe (2190°F)
5. **Orthoclase:** thin edges fuse with difficulty (2374°F)
6. **Enstatite:** only thinnest edges fuse with blowpipe (2550°F)
7. **Quartz:** no fusing at all in blowpipe flame (Over 2550°F)

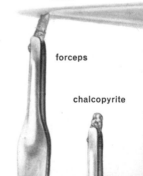

blowpipe flame

forceps

chalcopyrite

GEIGER COUNTERS are not tools for the amateur mineralogist but have become well known because of their use in locating or checking deposits of uranium and thorium. The Geiger tube is the heart of the counter. A wire down the centre of the tube has a negative charge. However, no current flows, because of the gas that fills the tube. When the tube is exposed to radiation, some of the molecules of the gas are ionized. They develop an electric charge because of electrons knocked from them. The ionized gas conducts electricity and there is a momentary flash of current through the tube. This is recorded on a counter or dial, or heard as a click in headphones. Cosmic rays from outer space also discharge the Geiger tube, and these must be considered when searching for ore. In order to get an effect, the ordinary Geiger counter must be held close to the ore. Hence it works best on outcrops and other exposed rock. The richer the ore, the more numerous the discharges and clicks. The scintillometre is another sensitive apparatus used to detect radioactive materials.

MINERALS as natural inorganic chemicals can be identified by their chemical properties as well as by hardness, streak, or lustre. Once a mineral is dissolved (often a difficult task), other chemical solutions can be added to identify the elements in it. Chemists make constant use of these "wet" tests. Although prospectors working in isolated places can frequently identify a mineral or rock by its physical properties, they also collect and bring material in for laboratory study.

Laboratory tests often involve a blowpipe, a short metal tube for blowing air into a flame. In blowpipe analysis, a bit of the mineral to be tested is heated on a charcoal block. The coloured coatings which form identify the elements present. The mineral may be powdered, also, and a touch of the powder absorbed in a drop of melted borax to give a bead test (p. 28). When mineral powder is brought into a flame, the flame colour may be studied. Powdered minerals are also heated in closed or open tubes (p. 30).

Mineral analysis calls for the basic materials listed below—as well as for a working knowledge of chemistry. Books to help you are listed on p. 156.

Blowpipe
Charcoal blocks
Spirit or gas burner
Test tubes
Open tubes
Chemical forceps
Platinum wire

Mortar and pestle
Blue and green glass
Hammer and small anvil
Litmus paper
Borax powder and other
  chemicals
Magnet

Use blowpipe to send a stream of air into flame, moulding it into a narrow cone about 2 in. long. For reducing flame, hold blowpipe behind flame and heat specimen at tip of interior bluish cone. For oxidizing flame, hold blowpipe in flame and heat specimen at tip.

BLOWPIPE TESTS make use of a spirit, gas, or candle flame. Moving the blowpipe back and forth as shown above produces an oxidizing flame (extra oxygen comes from the air blown into the flame) or a reducing flame (hot gases take oxygen from the specimen). The powdered specimen set in a hollow at one end of a charcoal block is heated in the flame until changes occur. Sometimes a fine, coloured coating (sublimate) forms; sometimes a bead of metal is left behind or characteristic fumes are released. When a flux (iodide, bromide, or chromate) is added to the powdered mineral, differently coloured coatings form. These may be used to confirm the tests. In some tests the mineral is heated on a block of plaster instead of a charcoal block. Finally, the blowpipe can be used to heat a mineral specimen directly, as in determining fusibility. A sliver of the mineral is held by forceps directly in the flame, as shown on p. 23.

Blowpipe test for zinc: heating ore on charcoal with oxidizing flame.

SAMPLE BLOWPIPE TESTS

for the metallic element in the mineral specimen:

Antimony forms a dense white coating, bluish at the fringe; it is volatile, but not as much as arsenic, which forms a similar coating and has a garlic odour.

ANTIMONY

BISMUTH

COPPER

LEAD

Bismuth minerals give an orange-yellow coating, which becomes greenish-yellow on cooling. A grey-brittle button of bismuth also forms. When iodide flux is mixed with the powdered mineral, the coating is yellow with a reddish border.

Copper When oxides are heated in the reducing flame with a flux practically no coating results, but a reddish ball of metallic copper remains. Blowpipe flame is coloured blue-green.

Lead minerals heated in a reducing flame leave behind a grey ball of metallic lead. The coating is yellowish (darker when hot) with a white or bluish border.

Zinc minerals give a small coating close to the specimen—bright yellow when hot (p. 26), white when cold. Add a drop of cobalt nitrate solution to the coating, reheat, and the coating will turn green. Use plaster block with iodide flux.

ZINC

Bead in oxidizing flame

BEAD TESTS

BEAD TESTS help identify metals when minerals are dissolved in a flux and heated. The flux is borax, heated in a loop of platinum wire till a clear glassy bead is formed. The hot borax bead is touched to a trace of the powdered mineral and is reheated in reducing and oxidizing flames. The colour of the bead is noted when hot and when cold. All traces of a previous bead must be "washed" off the wire before a new test is made. Below are the colours in some common bead tests.

Metal	OXIDIZING FLAME		REDUCING FLAME	
	Hot	Cold	Hot	Cold
Antimony	yellow	colourless	yellow	colourless
Chromium	yellow	green	green	green
Cobalt	blue	blue	blue	blue
Copper	green	blue	colourless	brown
Iron	yellow	green	green	green
Manganese	violet-brown	violet	colourless	colourless
Molybdenum	yellow	colourless	brown	brown
Nickel	violet	brown	colourless-grey	colourless-grey
Titanium	colourless	colourless-white	yellow-grey	yellow
Tungsten	yellow	colourless	yellow	brown
Uranium	yellow	yellow-brown	green	green
Vanadium	yellow	green	brown	green

After M. Zim, Blowpipe Analysis and Tests for Common Minerals, *1935.*

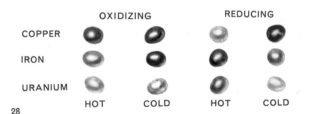

	OXIDIZING		REDUCING	
COPPER				
IRON				
URANIUM				
	HOT	COLD	HOT	COLD

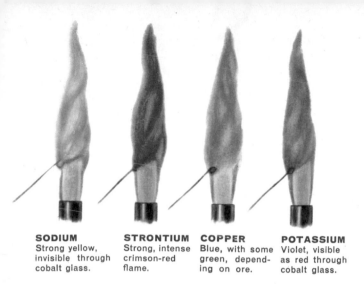

SODIUM
Strong yellow, invisible through cobalt glass.

STRONTIUM
Strong, intense crimson-red flame.

COPPER
Blue, with some green, depending on ore.

POTASSIUM
Violet, visible as red through cobalt glass.

FLAME TESTS depend on the fact that small amounts of mineral introduced into a flame will colour the flame, depending on the metals it contains. Flame tests are fairly crude, but when such flames are viewed through a spectroscope, a highly accurate kind of chemical analysis is possible. The spectroscope and the X-ray are important tools in advanced work with minerals and are essential in working with small, rare specimens.

To make simple flame tests, use a clean platinum or nichrome wire. The wire, dipped in strong hydrochloric acid, is held in the flame until no change in flame colour is seen. The wire loop is touched to a bit of the powdered mineral, also moistened with acid, and then flamed. The flame may be viewed directly, or through a cobalt blue glass, which masks the yellow sodium colour.

SULPHUR melts in closed tube test. On continued heating it forms a yellow to reddish-brown sublimate in the cool part of the tube.

LEAD ORE (galena) turns a light colour and forms a white sublimate when heated in an open tube.

TUBE TESTS involve heating powdered minerals in closed and open tubes to see what sublimates form in the upper, cooler part of the tube, and to notice fumes and odours from the heated mineral. The closed tube is an ordinary pyrex test tube. Use only enough mineral to barely cover the bottom. Hold at a low angle in Bunsen burner flame and heat until mineral is red hot. Watch for fumes and sublimates. The open tube can be a piece of straight or bent glass tubing about six inches long. The powdered mineral is inserted about an inch from the lower end, and the specimen is heated while being held at a low angle. Do not tilt higher or the specimen will spill. Air circulates through the open tube and oxidizes the mineral powder. Sublimates form at the cool end. Use a test tube holder for these tests.

METALLIC MINERALS

The metals are the core of our civilization. Life as we know it would be impossible without them. Here are the minerals from which our most important metals are obtained; they form an interesting group for collectors.

COPPER nuggets were found by ancient man. Later, copper was smelted from its ores. Today it is essential for practically all things electrical and for many other uses. Chile, Peru, Cyprus, Africa, Japan, and Australia have large deposits. British deposits are found in Cornwall. Copper occurs principally in volcanic rocks and in veins. Native copper (H. 2.5 to 3, Sp. Gr. 8.9) is hard to mine. The sulphides and carbonates described on the next page are easier to handle. Some malachite and azurite is cut for ornaments and gems, as is chrysocolla, a copper silicate. Cuprite (copper oxide), a reddish brown mineral, results from oxidation of other copper minerals. Sulphides are black, purple, and yellow. The oxide and native copper are dull red; the carbonates, blue and green. Crystals are rare.

NATIVE COPPER
in matrix

crystal

NATIVE COPPER

Chalcocite (Cu_2S) is a dark metallic mineral. H. 2.5; Sp. Gr. 5.5; streak, grey to black. An important ore, it is found with the other three minerals on this page. Usually occurs in vein deposits; crystals rare.

crystal

Covellite (CuS), found with other copper sulphide ores, forms thin deep blue plates, usually tarnished to purple or black. Not as common or as rich in copper as chalcocite. H. 1.5 to 2; Sp. Gr. 4.6; lustre, metallic. Occurs as crystals or incrustations.

Bornite (Cu_5FeS_4) is called peacock ore because of its usually shiny, purple tarnish. An important ore, found in veins or scattered in igneous rock. Crystals rare. Bronze-coloured when fresh. H. 3; Sp. Gr. 5; streak, black. May contain small amounts of gold and silver.

Chalcopyrite ($CuFeS_2$), the common copper ore, is a brassy, almost golden mineral. May form crystals but is more often found in massive form, in most copper mines. H. 3.5 to 4; Sp. Gr. 4.2; streak, greenish-black; very brittle.

Cuprite (Cu_2O) forms by weathering of other ores and so is more common near the surface. Cubic crystals fairly common. Also occurs as grains and irregular masses. H. 3.5; Sp. Gr. 6; colour, reddish brown; streak, brownish.

Chrysocolla ($CuSiO_3 \cdot 2H_2O$) is found in veins and masses with quartz in most copper mines in the Southwest. Its chief value is as a gem when even-coloured and rich in quartz. Colour varies, often bluish green; H. 2 to 4; Sp. Gr. 2. Crystals are rare.

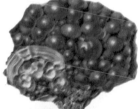

Malachite and Azurite are usually found together. Malachite ($CuCO_3 \cdot Cu(OH)_2$), more common than azurite, is various shades of green. Azurite ($2CuCO_3 \cdot Cu(OH)_2$), which is blue, forms crystals more often. Both occur in smooth or irregular masses in the upper levels of mines. Compact, deep-coloured stones are cut as ornaments. H. (for both) about 4; Sp. Gr. 3.7 to 4.

MALACHITE

AZURITE

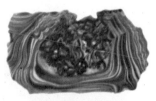

cut and polished

Azurite and malachite mixture

GALENA CRYSTALS

LEAD does occur as the native metal, but only rarely. The most important source of lead is the mineral galena, lead sulphide (PbS). It has been known for centuries, and lead, smelted easily from it, has also been used since ancient times. Galena is found in veins, pockets, and replacement deposits in carbonate rocks. It occurs with zinc, copper, and silver, often containing enough of the latter metals to make the ore doubly valuable.

Galena is a heavy, brittle, silvery-grey mineral which commonly forms cubic crystals and has perfect cubic cleavage. Its crystals were used in early radio sets. H. 2.5; Sp. Gr. 7.5; streak, lead-grey. The main deposits are found in Australia and North America; in Britain it was formerly mined in the South and Central Pennines, and in the south of Scotland.

CRYSTALS
AS MINED

cleavage planes

CERUSSITE

ANGLESITE REPLACING GALENA

CERUSSITE IN HEMATITE

Over a dozen other lead minerals exist, but of this number only two have much importance as ores. Both are secondary minerals derived from galena by the slow action of air and water. Silver-bearing galena is roasted to form lead oxide and sulphur dioxide gas, then reduced with carbon. Zinc is added. The silver and zinc rise and are skimmed off. The zinc is removed by distillation.

Cerussite ($PbCO_3$) forms large white or grey crystals, sometimes needle-like in bundles. It also occurs as massive deposits or as loose, crystalline crusts. H. 3; Sp. Gr. 6.5; adamantine or silky lustre; white streak.

Anglesite ($PbSO_4$) is often found with galena, as a white or grey crust. H. 3, Sp. Gr. 6.4; streak, white.

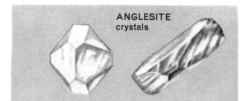

ANGLESITE
crystals

GOLD is neither the rarest nor the most valuable metal, yet it is part of the foundation of trade and commerce, and has many uses because of its metallic properties. Ancients who found native gold prized it, and gold, beautiful and easily worked, is still widely used in jewellery. A soft metal (H. 2.5), it is sometimes alloyed with copper to harden it and make it go further. Pure gold is 24 carats; hence 14 carat gold is 14/24 or about 60 per cent gold. Gold is found in quartz veins, sometimes with pyrite. The gold may occur within the pyrite itself—giving fool's gold a real value. Gold may occur in metamorphic rock and occasionally in sediments where it has been redeposited. Only rarely is visible gold found in gold ore. It usually cannot be seen at all. Some of the commercial ores contain only 0.1 ounce of gold for each ton of rock.

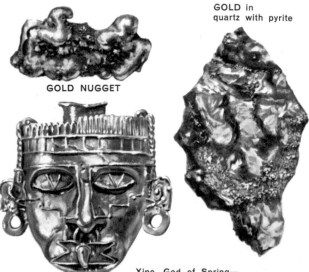

GOLD NUGGET

GOLD in
quartz with pyrite

Xipe, God of Spring—
ancient gold work from Mexico

Mining gold with sluice and pan

As gold deposits are eroded, the heavy gold (Sp. Gr. 19.3) is concentrated in stream beds where grains, flakes, and even nuggets may be found by washing away the lighter sand in a gold pan or a sluice. From these placer deposits miners have gone on to search for the original veins or "lodes". Here the gold may be found as flecks in the quartz and, rarely, as octahedral crystals. Gold is malleable; colour pale to golden yellow; metallic lustre. It occurs as a compound with tellurium in such minerals as sylvanite $(Au,Ag)Te_2$ and calaverite, $AuTe_2$. Gold may also be recovered from other metallic ores.

GOLD CRYSTAL 0.1 in.

GOLD ORE

ARGENTITE

crystal
0.3 in.

NATIVE SILVER

SILVER sometimes occurs as native silver in large twisting, branching masses. Another important source of silver is the sulphide (Ag_2S)—argentite. In addition, silver, lead, sulphur, and antimony form a whole series of rare, complex minerals. Silver may be a valuable by-product in smelting lead, zinc, and other metals.

Argentite is massive, or it may form cubic crystals. Found with lead, copper, and zinc minerals. Colour silvery when fresh, black to grey when tarnished. H. 2.5; Sp. Gr. 7.3; lustre, metallic.

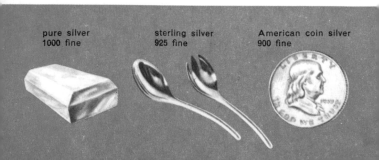

pure silver
1000 fine

sterling silver
925 fine

American coin silver
900 fine

MERCURY, in the form of cinnabar (HgS), is frequently a bright red, attractive mineral found near hot springs and in low-temperature veins—typically near volcanic rocks. The chief producing countries are Italy, the United States, and above all Spain, where the famous Almaden mine has been exploited since the time of the Carthaginians. Cinnabar forms hexagonal crystals but is usually massive or occurs as scattered flecks. H. 2.5; Sp. Gr. 8.1; colour varies from black to bright red; prismatic cleavage. Mercury is also found as silvery globules of native mercury in deposits of cinnabar. It is used in medicine, in the manufacture of thermometers and explosives, and in several chemical industries.

CINNABAR

0.1 in.

crystal

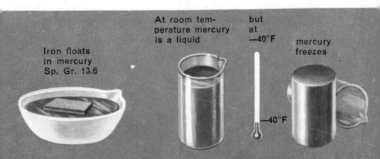

Iron floats in mercury Sp. Gr. 13.6

At room temperature mercury is a liquid

but at —40°F mercury freezes

—40°F

Toluca, Mexico

crystal

IRON ORES

METEORITES are "shooting stars" which reach the earth. Some are stony; others iron alloyed with nickel and traces of other metals. Meteors range from sand-grain size to masses weighing tons. Surface often pitted, oxidized, or rusty. Iron meteors are magnetic. H. 4 to 5; Sp. Gr. 7.5.

MAGNETITE (Fe_3O_4) is the only black ore that can be picked up easily by a magnet. The hard (H. 6) and heavy (Sp. Gr. 5.2) black crystals or masses are found in basic igneous rocks and metamorphosed sedimentary rocks. A valuable ore, though sometimes difficult to mine. Streak, black.

HEMATITE (Fe_2O_3), the most important iron ore, contains about 70 per cent iron. Great beds occur in the Great Lakes region of North America. Hematite varies from a red earthy powder to a dark, compact, shiny mineral. H. 1 to 6; Sp. Gr. about 5; streak, cherry red.

LIMONITE, an iron ore with water ($2Fe_2O_3 \cdot 3H_2O$), is soft and earthy (yellow ochre) or in compact, smooth, dark, rounded masses. Never crystalline. Limonite with about 60 per cent iron forms a series of very similar iron minerals. H. 1 to 5.5; Sp. Gr. about 3.5; streak, yellow-brown.

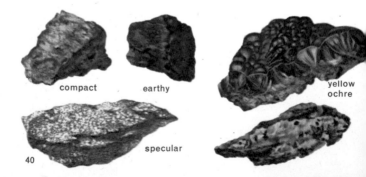

compact

earthy

specular

yellow ochre

crystal forms

MARCASITE (FeS_2), sometimes called white pyrites, is similar but lighter and more brittle than true pyrites. It occurs in radiating and coxcomb forms, as crustations and concretions, in clays, peat, common; streak, greyish or dark brown. Specimens crumble and break up on standing.

PYRITE (FeS_2) or fool's gold is not like gold at all, but when tarnished may resemble chalcopyrite (p. 32). Used to obtain sulphur and sometimes as a source of iron. Crystals are common; also occurs as grains or in masses. H. 6; Sp. Gr. about 5; streak, greenish—black; colour, brassy yellow.

PYRRHOTITE (FeS) varies in composition but always contains an excess of sulphur. Often found with nickel (pentlandite) and mined for its nickel content. Occurs as crystals, thin plates, grains, or masses. Colour, bronze (pyrite is brassy); H. 4; Sp. Gr. 4.6; streak, grey-black. Often magnetic.

SIDERITE ($FeCO_2$) is occasionally used as iron ore but deposits are usually small and iron content is low—48 per cent. Crystals common; more often in masses which cleave like calcite (p. 64). Colour, yellow, grey, dark brown; H. about 4; Sp. Gr. 3.8; streak, white; lustre, pearly.

crystal

ore + scrap + limestone + coke + air blast = pig iron

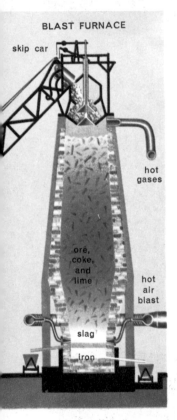

BLAST FURNACE

skip car

hot gases

ore, coke, and lime

hot air blast

slag

iron

Iron has long been man's most important metal. Continuously operating blast furnaces similar to the one shown are used to produce pig iron and ferro-alloys. The furnace is lined with fire brick not bound with mortar.

Iron ore is generally an oxide, as hematite, limonite, or magnetite, although occasionally a sulphide is used after conversion to an oxide by roasting. The ore is dumped into the furnace along with coke, and limestone for flux. Blasts of hot air roar in from the sides, uniting with the carbon of the coke to reduce the ore to metallic iron which flows to the bottom of the furnace, beneath the slag.

The furnaces are tapped regularly. Most of the molten iron is taken directly to Bessemer or open hearth converters to be made into steel. Some is run into moulds, making pig iron.

NICKEL ore, hard to smelt in the early days of European mining, was thought bewitched and was spurned by miners. The world's largest deposits are located near Sudbury, Ontario, which produces more than three-fourths of the world's nickel. Nickelite (NiAs) and millerite (NiS)

Open-pit mining

are minor nickel ores occurring with sulphide and arsenic ores of cobalt and iron. The principal ore of nickel (pentlandite) occurs in pyrrhotite (p. 41) and is similar to it. Greenish secondary ores are found near the surface, where weathering has altered the primary minerals. Nickel, a magnetic metal, is widely used in alloys, especially with iron. Permalloy and alnico, both nickel alloys, are used in making magnets. German silver, another alloy, is used for kitchenware, ornaments, and electrical heating wire. Cupronickel, an alloy of nickel and copper, is widely used for 'silver' coins (e.g. British shilling, florin & half-crown).

NICKELITE

COBALTITE

0.1 in.

CRYSTAL FORMS: cubic

0.1 in.

12-sided

SKUTTERUDITE

COBALT is chemically related to nickel and iron, and its ores are often found with nickel and iron minerals. The Belgian Congo and Zambia are the largest producers; there, the cobalt is found with copper. There are also large deposits of cobalt ores in the Scandinavian countries, and in Canada with nickel.

Cobaltite ($CoAsS$) and skutterudite $(CoNiFe)As_3$ (smaltite) are the chief ores at Cobalt, Ontario. Both crystallize in the cubic system and look alike. Cobaltite has a hardness of 5.5; colour, silver-metallic. Skutterudite, which is similar, also contains variable amounts of nickel and iron and is classified as an ore of whichever metal is dominant.

It is the source of colour in blue glass. Cobalt also has other chemical uses.

Cobalt is a heavy metal (Sp. Gr. 8.9) used in hardening steels and in other alloys. Carboloy, an alloy of cobalt and tungsten carbide, is used in cutting steel. Another ferro-cobalt alloy makes permanent magnets. Cobalt oxides are important pigments in paints and ceramics, in which they are used to produce shades of green, blue, yellow, and red.

TIN is seen daily as the thinner-than-paper coating on the surface of tin cans. This layer protects the iron of the can from rusting. About half the supply of tin goes into the 50 milliard tin cans made yearly. Tin is also an important constituent of bearing alloys (Babbitt metal) and of type metal and solder. In its oldest use, and still a major one, it is alloyed with copper and some zinc to make bronze.

Tin is essentially a one-ore metal. The ore, cassiterite (SnO_2), tin oxide, contains almost 80 per cent tin. It is commonly brown or black, though occasionally red, grey, or yellow. Streak, pale; lustre, glassy to adamantine. Cassiterite forms crystals, but occurs more often as fibrous masses (wood tin) or as crusts or veins in granite and pegmatite rock. It may be distinguished from limonite by its high specific gravity (7.0). The Malay placer deposits of gravel and cassiterite pebbles are mined by huge dredges. Small amounts occur in placer deposits in Alaska, but most tin comes from Malaysia and Bolivia. The Romans mined tin from placer deposits in Cornwall, England.

CASSITERITE

CASSITERITE—WOOD TIN

PLACER CASSITERITE

tin can

typemetal

bearings

solder

45

BLENDE

crystal 0.2 in.

FRANKLINITE
in calcite

ZINCITE, WILLEMITE,
AND FRANKLINITE

ZINC was used as an alloy with copper to produce brass long before it was known as a metallic element. Now zinc is widely used in coating iron to prevent rust (galvanized iron), as well as in dry-cell batteries, paints, other alloys and in chemical industries. Zinc ores occur with lead and copper ores in veins associated with igneous rocks (p. 109) and as replacement deposits in carbonate rocks.

Blende, zincblende, or blackjack (ZnS) is the primary mineral. Colour: yellow, brown, or black; lustre: resinous. H. 3.5-4. Sp. Gr. 4. Blende has perfect cleavage and breaks easily. Some specimens are fluorescent; others emit flashes of light when scratched in a dark room.

Zincite is orange-red zinc oxide (ZnO). Found with frank-linite, a mineral similar to magnetite, containing zinc and manganese.

Smithsonite ($ZnCO_3$) forms as zinc ores weather. It is often a crystalline crust but mostly earthy and dull.

Hemimorphite ($Zn_4Si_2O_7(OH)_2 \cdot H_2O$), a zinc silicate with water, forms crystals or earthy deposits.

Willemite (Zn_2SiO_4), translucent, varies in colour. Often fluorescent (p. 22).

SMITHSONITE ON GALENA

SMITHSONITE

HEMIMORPHITE

WILLEMITE

ALUMINIUM

hardness 5

hardness 7

Kyanite, or cyanite ($Al_2 SiO_5$), is usually found in schists and gneisses. The white to blue-grey or black crystals are long and blade-like. Lustre, glassy to pearly; Sp. Gr. 3.6; hardness unusual—4 to 5 along the crystal axis, but 7 across.

Cryolite (Na_3AlF_6) is a rare mineral. Small amounts have been found in Colorado, but it is the one great deposit in Greenland that was crucial in the history of aluminium making the smelting of bauxite possible. Now, artificial cryolite is used. H. 2.5; Sp. Gr. 3; glassy or greasy lustre. Splinters fuse in candle flame.

Corundum (Al_2O_3) is a primary aluminium mineral found in metamorphosed limestones and in schists. Hexagonal crystals common. Corundum also occurs as dark granules with magnetite – a form known as emery and used as an abrasive. H. 9—harder than any other common mineral; Sp. Gr. 4; colour variable.

crystal

Emery

MINERALS

Bauxite, the ore of aluminium, is a group of related oxides with water ($Al_2O_3 \cdot 2H_2O$). Most abundant in warmer areas, it forms as aluminium-bearing rocks are weathered. Colour, white — though often stained brown or red by iron oxides. H., variable, 1 to 3; Sp. Gr., 2.5. It is named after the region near Baux in France where it occurs. The Guianas have rich deposits.

Kaolin, a group of at least three minerals, all aluminium silicates with water ($H_4Al_2Si_2O_9$), is white and scaly when pure. More often found impure as clay; then it is earthy and coloured by impurities. Kaolin is widespread, though pure deposits are limited. The China clay of southwestern England is the product of the alteration of granites. It is essential in ceramics and has many other uses. It is also a potential source of metallic aluminium, though commercial smelting methods are yet to be developed.

BAUXITE

KAOLIN

CRYSTALLINE KAOLIN
(highly magnified)

49

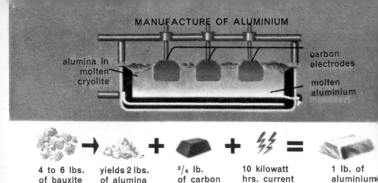

alumina in molten cryolite

carbon electrodes

molten aluminium

| 4 to 6 lbs. of bauxite | yields 2 lbs. of alumina | $3/4$ lb. of carbon | 10 kilowatt hrs. current | 1 lb. of aluminium |

ALUMINIUM, as a commercial metal, has been known for over a hundred years, but its wide use has been much more recent. Clays containing aluminium were used in making pottery long before metals were known. Pottery and other ceramic products still utilize large quantities of aluminium minerals (p. 150). Aluminium is a constituent of feldspars, micas, garnets, corundum, and cryolite, but only the latter has ever been an aluminium ore. Aluminium ores are usually secondary—weathered and altered products of these minerals.

Aluminium, making up over 8 per cent of the earth's crust, is more abundant than iron, but workable deposits are limited. Bauxite, consisting of hydrated oxides of aluminium, is the principal ore. In processing, the 50 to 70 per cent aluminium oxide, called alumina, is first extracted, then dissolved in huge vats of molten cryolite. Alumina is reduced to metallic aluminium by carbon electrodes carrying a strong electric current. It collects at the bottom of the vat. About a million tons a year are produced, mainly for the transportation and construction industries.

Pouring molten aluminium

CHROMIUM, a bright silvery metal, has become familiar in the flashy trim on automobiles and household wares. It is often used over a nickel undercoat as a non-rusting plating on iron and steel. Chromium has only one ore, though it occurs in about a dozen minerals.

CHROMITE

Chromite ($FeCr_2O_4$), the chromium ore, occurs widely, in Africa, the Philippines, Turkey, and New Caledonia. Chromite occurs in basic igneous rocks or in metamorphic rocks formed from them. Chromite (H. 5.5; Sp. Gr. 4.7) is metallic black or brownish; streak, dark brown. Sometimes slightly magnetic because of its iron content, it occurs in veins or in widespread granular masses, frequently with a coating of serpentine.

CHROMITE
crystal

Crocoite ($PbCrO_4$), a rare but handsome mineral, is formed when chrome chemicals encounter lead. Attractive crystals of lead chromate then develop.

CROCOITE

51

MANGANESE is widely found, often with iron, barium, cobalt, and zinc. The most common ores are secondary, formed by the action of air and water on manganese silicates and carbonates. Deposits are common in bogs and lakes. Manganese is used to toughen steel for machinery, rails, and armaments. Russia, India, South Africa, and Brazil have most of the ores.

Rhodonite ($MnSiO_3$)—pink, yellow, or brownish—is best known from Franklin Furnace, N.J. H. 5.5 to 6.5; Sp. Gr. 3.5; translucent; streak, white. Large, flattened crystals quite common. Prismatic cleavage.

Rhodochrosite ($MnCO_3$), softer than rhodonite (H. 4), rarely forms large crystals. Translucent with glassy lustre; colour pinkish, as in rhodonite. Massive, in veins or as crusts. Typical calcite cleavage (rhombohedral).

Psilomelane ($MnO_2 \cdot H_2O$) appears often with barium and iron. Soft, dull, non-crystalline (see manganite, below), but may form hard (H. 5) rounded or stringy masses. Soft, impure mixtures are called wad.

Manganite, $MnO(OH)$, is often in prismatic crystals or fibrous masses. H. 4; Sp. Gr. 4.3; streak, red-brown.

Pyrolusite (MnO_2), principal manganese ore, is earthy, powdery, granular, or fibrous. Hardness varies from 1 or 2 up to 6 in rare crystals. Sp. Gr. 5; streak, black. Forms fernlike crusts (dendrites) along cracks or as inclusions in moss agate. These are not fossils.

MOSS AGATES

Pyrolusite dendrites in quartz

RHODONITE

RHODOCHROSITE

PSILOMELANE

MANGANITE

PYROLUSITE DENDRITES
on dolomite

PYROLUSITE

crystal
forms   0.1 in.

URANINITE

PITCHBLENDE

URANIUM (discovered in 1789 and isolated as an element about 1842) is now prized as a source of atomic energy. It occurs in some 50 minerals, most of them rare. The main ores are uraninite and secondary minerals formed from it by weathering. Actually, uranium minerals are widespread in granites and pegmatites. Specimens may be collected wherever these igneous rocks are exposed. Commercial deposits are another matter. Uranium prospecting requires time, patience, and skills which few amateur mineralogists possess.

Uraninite (UO_2) is steel black, opaque, hard (H. 5.5), and heavy; Sp. Gr. 9 to 9.5 for pure specimens. Streak from grey to brown to black; crystals rare. More common is **pitchblende,** a form of uraninite which occurs in massive, fibrous or rounded masses.

Uraninite alters to an orange or red gummy, waxy mineral of variable composition, called gummite.

Carnotite ($K_2(UO_2)_2(VO_4)_2 \cdot 3H_2O$) is a complex mineral with vanadium and uranium. It occurs in weathered sedimentary rocks as streaks or earthy yellow grains.

Uranophane ($CaU_2Si_2O_{11} \cdot 7H_2O$) is found with uraninite as clusters of tiny yellow, needle-like crystals. It is widely distributed, but never common.

Autunite ($Ca(UO_2)_2(PO_4)_2 \cdot 10\text{-}12H_2O$) is another secondary uranium mineral. Note the greenish, pearly flecks. Autunite is common in small amounts. This and most other uranium minerals fluoresce strongly under ultraviolet light. Radiation from these minerals can also be detected by the use of a Geiger counter or a scintillometre.

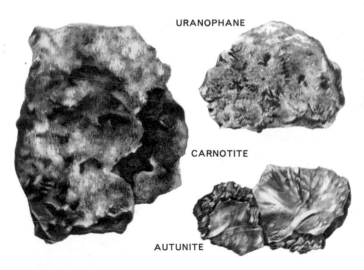

URANOPHANE

CARNOTITE

AUTUNITE

WOLFRAMITE

SCHEELITE

VANADINITE

MOLYBDENITE

IMPORTANT MINOR METALS

Wolframite $(Fe,Mn)WO_2$ is a mineral of quartz veins and pegmatites. It is found in the form of tabular or prismatic crystals; dark brown or black with submetallic lustre; H. 5.5; Sp. Gr. 7.5; brittle. An ore of tungsten (wolfram)—important in lamp filaments and in steel-alloy cutting tools.

Scheelite $(CaWO_4)$, another ore of tungsten. H. 5; Sp. Gr. 6. Glassy, sometimes transparent; streak, white. Colour variable, but light. Found in quartz veins or at contact of igneous rocks and limestone. It is the most important U.S. tungsten ore.

Vanadinite $(Pb_5(VO_4)_3Cl)$ is an attractive, fairly widespread vanadium mineral, but not an important ore. H. 3; Sp. Gr. 7. Vanadinite is a secondary mineral of lead areas. Carnotite (p. 55) is a better source of vanadium, used in alloy steels.

Molybdenite (MoS_2) is a mineral found in pegmatites and veins. It is soft (H. 1.5), metallic and opaque; streak, blue-grey. Occurs as flecks, or tabular crystals. Molybdenum is essential in tool-steel alloys.

Columbite $(Fe,Mn)Cb_2O_6$ and **tantalite** $(Fe,Mn)Ta_2O_6$ are ores of rare metals. Actually, they are a series of oxides including iron and manganese. The mineral is columbite when the amount of columbium (niobium) is high, and tantalite when it has more tantalum, which is used as an alloy in surgical instruments. Columbium alloys are used in rocket engines.

COLUMBITE AND TANTALITE

The minerals are dark brown or black, crystalline (often twinned). H. 6; Sp. Gr. 5.5 to 8; usually opaque with a submetallic lustre. They form in pegmatite, often with tin and tungsten minerals.

Beryl $(Be_3Al_2(SiO_3)_6$ is an ore of beryllium as well as a gem stone (pp. 84-85). The metal is used in alloys of copper and in atomic research. It is almost as light as magnesium.

BERYL

Monazite, H. 5; Sp. Gr. 5, is a complex mineral containing thorium and a number of other "rare earth" metals. It occurs as yellow resinous grains or as larger crystals in pegmatite and in certain sand deposits in India and the south-eastern United States. An even greater number of "rare earths" are found in **samarskite**, which occurs rarely in pegmatites.

MONAZITE

SAMARSKITE

TITANIUM (Ti) is a light and very strong metal, used as a component of certain special steels. As an oxide it is also used in paint (titanium white), but it is in its metallic form that its use is most likely to develop. With its ability to withstand heat and its extreme lightness (Sp. Gr. 1.7), it would seem obviously indicated for use in aircraft and rocket construction.

Titanium is an abundant metal, forming 0.6% of the earth's crust. The chief mines being worked at present are situated in the U.S., India, Norway and Brazil.

Ilmenite (H. 5-6; Sp. Gr. 4.5) is the principal component of titanium ore. It is found, mixed with magnetite, in metamorphic rocks, in the form of blackish masses with a metallic lustre and forming a black or red-brown dust. Sometimes it is also found in granular form or as tabular crystals. But it is chiefly as "black dust", in river or sea alluvial deposits, that it is exploited.

Rutile (TiO_2), the oxide of titanium (H. 6; Sp. Gr. 4.2) is a black mineral, often in prismatic crystals with a pale brown dust. It is found in metamorphic rocks, but its principal deposits occur in sandy beaches in Australia. It can also occur as inclusions in quartz in igneous rocks (p. 78).

Ilmenite crystal

Titanium alloys used in rockets

Ilmenite

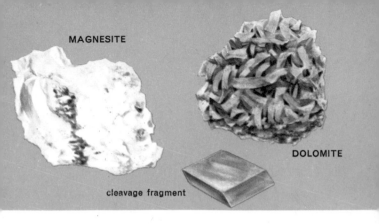

MAGNESITE

DOLOMITE

cleavage fragment

MAGNESIUM, lighter than aluminium, is the eighth most common element in the earth's crust. It has become a metal of major importance—its alloys find wide use in aeroplanes, in other sheet metal products, and in casting. Its two principal ores are magnesite and dolomite. Magnesium is also manufactured from sea water— 260,000 gallons yielding one ton of the metal. The magnesium chloride is treated with lime from oyster shells. Then the magnesium is extracted by electrolytic action.

Magnesite ($MgCO_3$), usually dull white, massive or granular, sometimes glassy, rarely occurs as crystals. H. 4; Sp. Gr. 3. Large deposits in Washington and California.

Dolomite ($MgCa(CO_3)_2$) is described as a non-metallic mineral (p. 65), but recently it has come into use as an ore of magnesium—just as the clay minerals may eventually become ores of aluminium. Three light metals— aluminium, magnesium, and lithium—are of growing importance.

Spinel, a magnesium-aluminium oxide, is a well-known gem mineral (p. 85) which is found mainly in Ceylon, Burma, and Thailand.

STIBNITE

STIBNITE, (Sb_2S_3), found with pyrite, galena, and arsenic minerals, is the only common antimony ore. It is more typical of low-temperature veins. Steel-grey, metallic; H. 2; Sp. Gr. 4.5. Crystals common, often found bent. Antimony is used in type metal, pewter, and other alloys. Native antimony is also found as a mineral—but rarely.

ARSENIC is a semi-metal used in alloys. Its poisonous compounds are used in sprays and insecticides.

Realgar (AsS), the simplest ore, forms in low-temperature veins as crusts, grains, flecks, or massive deposits. Crystals are rare. H. 2; Sp. Gr. 3.5; resinous lustre; colour and streak both orange-red. Realgar slowly breaks down on exposure to light to form orpiment.

Orpiment (As_2S_3), often found with realgar or stibnite, is usually massive, though sometimes sheet-like. Crystals rare. H. 1.5; Sp. Gr. 3.5; perfect cleavage. Specimens become dull on exposure to light.

Arsenopyrite (FeAsS) forms in high-temperature veins and pegmatites. Occurs massive or as crystals. Silvery, metallic; H. 6; Sp. Gr. 6. An ore of arsenic.

ORPIMENT

ARSENOPYRITE

REALGAR

NON-METALLIC MINERALS

NON-METALLIC MINERALS form a large group of minerals which contain no metal or are not used for the metals they contain. Gems and rock-forming minerals are in separate sections. Even a few metallic minerals (pp. 31-60) belong in the non-metallic group, for while they contain metals, they are not ores. The non-metallic minerals are of great importance—for insulation, as fillers, filters, and fluxes, and in the ceramic and chemical industries. The world's most common minerals belong in this group.

SULPHUR (S) is a non-metallic mineral element found in volcanic rocks, around hot springs, and in sedimentary "domes" (p. 145) with salt, gypsum, anhydrite, and limestone. It is yellow (sometimes brown), waxy or resinous, weak and brittle. H. 1.5 to 2.5; Sp. Gr. 2.0. Sulphur's low melting point (110-120°C) aids in mining it from underground deposits. Superheated water is pumped down large pipes, melting the sulphur; compressed air then forces the melted sulphur out. Sulphur is used in papermaking and as a source of sulphuric acid.

SULPHUR
on calcite

crystal

MASSIVE GRAPHITE

crucible

pencils

lubricant

motor brushes

GRAPHITE is one of the world's softest minerals. Diamond is the hardest. Both are carbon (C). Graphite occurs in igneous and metamorphic rocks—schists and marbles. It may form when high temperature veins cut coal deposits, and an artificial form is made in electric furnaces. Graphite is earthy, or forms scaly or flaky crystals with a metallic lustre, greasy and flexible. H. 1; Sp. Gr. 2.0. There are rich deposits in Korea, Ceylon, Mexico, and Madagascar. Graphite is used for dry and wet lubrication and for electrical and chemical purposes. Its best-known use is as "lead" in lead pencils, where it is usually mixed with other materials to give various degress of hardness. Graphite is a strategic mineral. Its latest use is as a moderator to slow down neutrons in atomic reactors.

Iceland Spar is a transparent calcite which has the optical property of bending light two ways, making words appear double.

Dogtooth Spar, a common crystalline form, with crystals long and pointed.

CALCITE

ICELAND SPAR

TWINNED CRYSTALS

Twinned Crystals of calcite, growing together as shown below (left) are very common. This is a typical spectacular form.

Stalactites and Stalagmites form in caves by dripping water. Calcite also forms in thin sheets or curtains from the roof.

CALCITE ($CaCO_3$), most common and widespread of the carbonate minerals, is interesting because of its many and varied crystal forms. Calcite occurs in a number of structural forms and frequently grades into dolomite (p. 65). Great masses of calcite occur in limestones (pp. 126-127); small crystal masses are present in rock openings, while rare, transparent crystals occur as Iceland spar, valued for use in range finders and polarizing microscopes. Calcite also occurs as a vein mineral In almost all rocks. Crystals are common. H. 3; Sp. Gr. 2.7. Cleavage: perfect, rhombohedral. Most calcite is opaque, slightly coloured by impurities; yellow, orange, brown, and green shades occur. Calcite is often fluorescent.

Other Forms of Calcite

Nail-head Spar: flattened, rhombohedral crystals, often in clusters.

Travertine: a general term for massive, non-crystalline calcite as found in caves. Opaque, often coloured.

Tufa: porous, white travertine from spring deposits.

Chalk: white, soft, compact shells of small sea animals.

BLUE CALCITE   TRAVERTINE

CALCITE SAND CRYSTALS

ARAGONITE CRYSTALS   PRECIOUS CORAL   ARAGONITE CRYSTAL

ARAGONITE is chemically the same as calcite ($CaCO_3$) but is less common and crystallizes in the orthorhombic system. It is slightly harder and heavier—H. 3.5 to 4; Sp. Gr. 2.9. Aragonite does not cleave as distinctly as calcite, although it, too, bubbles strongly in dilute hydrochloric acid. Aragonite is usually white, grey, or cream. The mother-of-pearl lining of sea shells is aragonite. **Flos ferri** is a branching growth of pure white aragonite in mines and caves. **Coral,** formed by animals in warm seas, is also aragonite. Precious coral is valued for gem and ornamental use.

DOLOMITE ($MgCa(CO_3)_2$) occurs in large bedded deposits and as veins in other sediments. There are extensive deposits in the Austrian Tyrol—the Dolomite Alps. Dolomite is both a rock and a mineral (p. 109). The best mineral specimens come from veins or limestone cavities, and include crystals with curved faces. Dolomite is harder than calcite (H. 3.5 to 5; Sp. Gr. 2.8), but similar in crystal form and cleavage. Reacts slowly with hydrochloric acid. White or varicoloured. Widely distributed.

DOLOMITE CRYSTALS

crystal

fishtail twins

curved crystal

GYPSUM is a common min-neral. It is a sedimentary rock precipitated from evaporating sea water under dry or arid con-ditions. Gypsum is the basis of a multimillion-pound indus-try producing plaster, plaster-board, rock lath, and other con-struction materials. A small amount of gypsum in Portland cement keeps it from setting too fast.

Gypsum was known and used in Europe for centuries. It was first burned in open fires, later in kilns. Heating gypsum drives out part of the water; the bur-ned gypsum, ground to a white powder, is known as plaster of Paris, as it was first made near there. When moistened, plaster of Paris absorbs water again and hardens as gypsum rock, so it is used in making plaster casts and in plastering and as an ingredient of many prepared construction materials.

Crushed gypsum is used in agriculture, being added to the soil as "land plaster". It aids the growth of peas and neutra-lizes alkaline soils.

Gypsum is a colourless or white mineral, sometimes tinted by iron or other impurities. It is calcium sulphate, with water (Ca$SO_4 \cdot 2H_2O$). H. 2; Sp. Gr. 2.3. Lustre is pearly, glassy—sometimes fibrous. Streak, white. Its crystals have two cleavage planes—one perfect. Does not bubble in cold hydrochloric acid, but will dissolve in hot.

Most gypsum occurs in bedded deposits. A compact massive form known as alabaster (a name also applied to similar-looking calcite) is carved for ornaments. Crystalline gypsum (selenite) occurs in caves and limestone cavities — also in clays, shales, and some sands. Crystals may grow several feet long, and may be twinned or curved.

Anhydrite ($CaSO_4$) is chemically similar to gypsum, but does not contain water. It is found in crystalline masses, though good crystals are rare. Sometimes it is fibrous, granular or scaly. Colour white to grey; streak, white. Lustre, glassy or pearly, often translucent, rarely transparent. H. 3 to 3.5; Sp. Gr. 2.9. It is often found with gypsum, and may alter to gypsum by absorbing water. Also occurs in salt beds and with sulphur in "domes".

MASSIVE GYPSUM

FIBROUS GYPSUM

ANHYDRITE

crystal

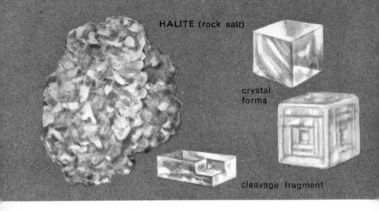

HALITE (rock salt)

crystal forms

cleavage fragment

HALITE or common salt is sodium chloride (NaCl). It has been used since prehistoric days, and there is no substitute for it in nutrition or in industry. All halite comes from the sea. Layers of rock salt mark areas where seas dried up in ancient times. In many places salt is still made by evaporating sea water in shallow basins.

Halite is colourless when pure, but is usually discoloured some shade of yellow, red, grey, or brown. It is transparent to translucent, brittle, and with excellent cleavage parallel to its crystal faces. H. 2 to 2.5; Sp. Gr. 2.3. It occurs in granular, fibrous, or crystalline masses, easily recognized by the cubic crystals and by the mineral's familiar taste. Halite is rarely pure. It occurs with other salts of calcium and magnesium.

GLAUBERITE, a sulphate of sodium and calcium, occurs around mineral springs and with other evaporites. H. 2.5; white to grey.

SALTPETRE, a fertilizer, is sodium nitrate ($NaNO_3$). It occurs in Chile and south-west U.S.A.— with gypsum, halite, and glauberite.

Salt mine

Salt and Related Minerals are part of the "alkali" which makes some soils difficult to use for agriculture. These minerals form under semi-arid to arid conditions, often with borax (p. 70). Halite is mined by shaft mining or by pumping water into the deposit and later pumping out the brine. In purification, potassium and magnesium salts, bromine, and iodine are obtained as by-products. The halite is recrystallized, becoming very pure in the process. In addition to its use in food and as a preservative, salt is essential in chemical industries, in the manufacture of soda ash for glass products, and in soapmaking and metallurgy. Chlorine from salt is used as a bleach and in water purification.

"Twenty-mule team" hauling borax.

BORAX, originally obtained from deposits of volcanic origin, now comes mostly from brines and dry lake beds where ground water has concentrated the borax. Used in making glass and enamels and in chemical industries.

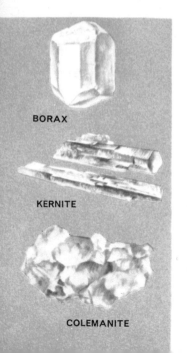

BORAX

KERNITE

COLEMANITE

Borax, sodium borate with ten parts of water, occurs in alkali lakes or as a crust on the desert soil. Once hauled in twenty-mule teams from the Death Valley region, California. White to grey; H. 2; Sp. Gr. 2.7; glassy.

Kernite is chemically similar to borax but contains only four parts of water. It is often colourless and transparent. H. 2.5; Sp. Gr. 2.0. Streak, white. Lustre, glassy.

Colemanite is a calcium borate with five parts of water. Prismatic crystals common. Colour, white. H. 4 to 4.5; Sp. Gr. 2.3. Streak, white. Lustre, glassy to dull. Often found in white, chalky or hard, glassy masses.

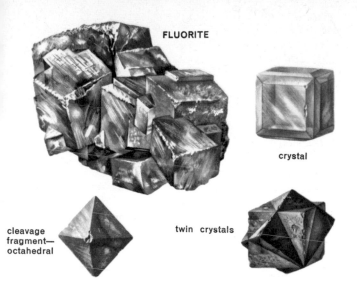

FLUORITE

crystal

cleavage fragment—octahedral

twin crystals

FLUORITE in commercial quantities occurs in both sedimentary and igneous rocks. Veins of fluorite (CaF_2) with quartz or calcite sometimes contain lead, copper and zinc minerals. The United States is the world's largest producer of fluorite; in Britain it is found widely in the Pennines. Fluorite is used to produce a fluid slag in steel-making and in smelting ores. It is used in making high-octane fuels, Freon, and many other chemical products. Fluorite is a most attractive mineral of varied colours—white, blue, green, and violet. Transparent to translucent. H. 4; Sp. Gr. 3.2. Streak, white; glassy lustre. Good octahedral cleavage. Crystals and fine cleavage fragments make attractive specimens for the collector. Often fluorescent in ultraviolet light.

BARITE or barytes ($BaSO_4$) is a sulphate of barium, a silvery metal. It is placed with the non-metallics because it is rarely a source of the metal and is widely used otherwise. Barite occurs in many ways, occasionally as large transparent or translucent crystals; sometimes as crystalline vein fillings, with fluorite or calcite, or with metallic ores. Large concretions are found in South Dakota and smaller rose-shaped ones ("desert roses") in the sands of Oklahoma.

Barite is a fairly soft (H. 2.5 to 3.5) but heavy (Sp. Gr. 4.5) mineral, colourless to white, yellow, grey, and brown. Lustre, glassy, sometimes pearly; streak, white. Sometimes granular or earthy. Crystals are common, often broad and thick. Barite is used in making lithopone for paint, as an aid in well drilling, in making glass, as a filler in glossy paper, and in ceramics.

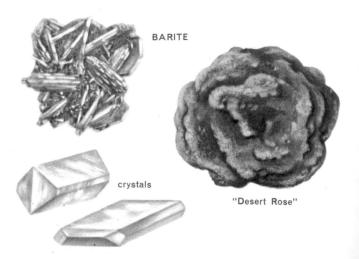

BARITE

crystals

"Desert Rose"

MASSIVE APATITE

APATITE CRYSTALS
in calcite

APATITE gets its odd name from the Greek word meaning "to deceive" because its varied forms and colours caused early mineralogists to confuse it with a half-dozen other minerals. Apatite may be transparent, translucent, or opaque, with a colour that varies from white to brown, green, yellow, or violet. Apatite occurs in veins with quartz, feldspar, and iron ores. Hexagonal crystals are common, some similar to gem minerals. Apatite is a phosphate of calcium, usually with some fluorine (Ca_5 (Cl,F)-$(PO_4)_3$). H. 5; Sp. Gr. 3.2; lustre, glassy; streak, white. Outstanding commercial deposits are present in Ontario and Quebec, Canada. Phosphate rock, used for fertilizer, contains minerals related to apatite. A thin chip of apatite will colour a gas flame orange (1). When wet with sulphuric acid (*caution!*) it colours the flame a pale bluish-green (2) due to liberated phosphorus.

FOLIATED TALC

GRANULAR TALC

STEATITE

TALC may form when magnesium-rich rocks are altered, especially by heated waters. Hence talc occurs as a secondary mineral with serpentine (p. 107), chlorite (p. 106), schists, and dolomite. It is found in irregular deposits in metamorphic rocks. Talc has a variety of uses ranging from cosmetics (talcum powder) to fillers in paint, insecticides, rubber, and paper. The use depends on the form in which the talc occurs—this may be massive, fibrous, or soft.

Soapstone is rock usually rich in talc. **Steatite** is a massive talc, usually of high grade. Talc is frequently sheet-like (foliated) or granular. As a mineral, it is one of the softest (H. 1 to 1.5), Sp. Gr. 2.7. Foliated talc has good basal cleavage and breaks somewhat like mica, though the scales are not elastic. Translucent to opaque; colour varies from white to greenish, yellow, or pink. Pure talc has a greasy, soapy feel and when powdered acts as a lubricant.

Talc and soapstone were known in ancient times. Eskimos carved lamps and pots from it, as did the Mound Builders. The Egyptians, Babylonians, and Chinese also made use of it.

ASBESTOS is the name given to a group of minerals different in origin but of similar appearance. Originally the term was applied to fibrous minerals closely related to amphibole (p. 100). Of the fibrous amphiboles, **crocidolite** or blue asbestos is best known. Mountain leather is a heavy, matted form; its fibres are usually short and brittle.

CROCIDOLITE ASBESTOS

The best-known source of asbestos is a form of serpentine (p. 107) known as **chrysotile.** It is silky, fibrous, and strong. Most chrysotile comes from the famous Quebec and Vermont deposits, where it honeycombs the serpentine rock. Here the cross fibres vary from ½ to 3 inches in length. The long fibres are in short supply and are valued very highly. The United States uses about 50 per cent of all asbestos produced; 90 per cent of this comes from Canada.

CHRYSOTILE ASBESTOS

Chrysotile fibres are so fine they can be divided into almost invisible strands. They spin well and are used in woven insulation and for fireproofing. The fibres do not burn and they conduct heat very slowly. Shorter fibres are mixed with gypsum to make asbestos board. Sight identification of chrysotile is easy —no other mineral is this fibrous.

LONG-FIBRED CHRYSOTILE

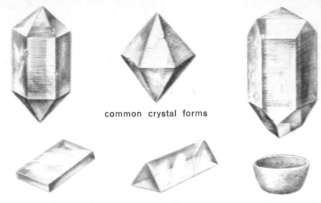

common crystal forms

quartz radio crystals   quartz prism   silica crucible

QUARTZ is one of the most common minerals in the earth's crust. As the chemical silica (SiO_2) it forms an important part of most igneous rocks. Some sandstones are almost 100 per cent quartz, and so are such metamorphic rocks as quartzite. At different temperatures quartz crystallizes in different ways. For this reason its crystal structure is often an aid in determining the temperature conditions under which a rock formed, since one variety, alpha-quartz, changes to another, beta-quartz, at 573°C.

Quartz occurs in crystalline masses and, when conditions permit, forms hexagonal crystals (pp. 78-79). Doubly terminated quartz crystals are often found. Larger crystals are found lining cavities; they are often cut as gem stones and are sold as rock crystal. Brazil is famous for its deposits of crystal quartz. Quartz also occurs in a form in which the crystals are of microscopic size and hence not apparent (pp. 80-81). Silica combined with water is opal (p. 82).

Quartz is sometimes colourless but more commonly white, sometimes yellow, brown, pink, green, blue, or black. Its lustre is glassy in crystalline forms, waxy or greasy in chalcedony. H. 7; Sp. Gr. 2.6; streak, white; brittle with conchoidal fracture. Quartz is best recognized by its hardness, lustre, and occurrence, and by its crystal form when evident. Many kinds of quartz are valued as gems and are classed as semiprecious stones.

When crystal quartz is cut at an exact angle to its axis, pressure on it generates a minute electrical charge. This effect makes quartz of great usefulness in radio, television, and radar. The supply of natural radio quartz is so limited that methods for growing quartz crystals in the laboratory have been developed. Quartz transmits short light waves (ultraviolet) better than glass. When not of radio quality, crystal quartz is melted to form blanks to make special lenses and prisms. Optical quartz can be made only from crystals. Less clear quartz is fused to make laboratory ware that is highly resistant to chemical action. Quartz sand is used in making glass.

Rock crystal on drusy quartz (crust of small crystals).

CRYSTALLINE QUARTZ is the most common kind, though well-developed clear crystals are rare. Rock crystal (colourless crystal quartz) makes a fine gem. The colours in crystal quartz may in part be due to impurities (manganese, iron, nickel) or to radium activity, as in smoky quartz; some disappear when the quartz is heated. The crystals often include air bubbles and traces of other minerals. Hairlike crystals of rutile form rutilated quartz or sagenite. Cat's eye and tiger's eye may contain fibres of asbestos. Ferruginous quartz is coloured by hematite.

ROSE QUARTZ occurs in crystalline masses—rarely as individual crystals. Some rose quartz is asteriated—that is, the cut stone reflects or transmits light in a star-like pattern. The colour is probably due to traces of manganese.

BLUE QUARTZ is an uncommon variety, different from the violet amethyst. It is found in the Blue Ridge Mountains, and with blue feldspar in the Smokies of North America.

CITRINE is a yellow quartz also called false topaz because of its colour. Good crystals of gem quality come from Brazil. Not to be confused with pale smoky quartz.

AMETHYST colour may be due to traces of manganese. Deeper coloured specimens are cut as gems. Once highly prized, amethyst lost much of its value ofter the great Brazilian deposits were found.

SMOKY QUARTZ, also called cairngorm or Scots topaz, varies in colour from smoky yellow to brown and black. The latter form is called morion. A well-known Scots gem stone, though also found and prized elsewhere.

MILKY QUARTZ, found in veins, is the most common crystalline quartz. It is translucent to opaque and is not often used as a gem.

QUARTZ WITH INCLUSIONS

tiger's eye   with rutile

ROSE QUARTZ

AMETHYST

SMOKY QUARTZ

BLUE QUARTZ

CAIRNGORM (MORION)

CITRINE QUARTZ

MILKY QUARTZ

CRYPTOCRYSTALLINE QUARTZ merely means quartz with hidden or microscopic crystals, in contrast to the varieties described on the preceding page. This group includes the chalcedonies and the flints, cherts, and jaspers. Most of these are translucent or opaque; some are colourful and are prized as gems.

CHALCEDONY is a group term for a waxy, smooth form of quartz often lining cavities, filling cracks or forming crusts. Sometimes transparent, usually translucent, Colours from white to grey, blue, brown, or black.

CARNELIAN (sard) is a clear chalcedony, usually some shade of red or reddish brown.

JASPER is an opaque quartz usually red, yellow, or brown, or a mixture of these colours. Sometimes banded. May grade into chert.

FLINT is a grey, brown, or black quartz frequently found as nodules in chalk. Duller, more opaque and rougher than chalcedony, it breaks with conchoidal fracture, producing sharp edges. Widely used by early man for making tools.

CHRYSOPRASE is a translucent, apple-green chalcedony; colouring due to nickel oxide.

AGATE is chalcedony with a banded or irregular, variegated appearance. Bands may be wavy or parallel, from differences in deposition. Petrified wood is usually an agatised wood. Agate may be artificially coloured. See p. 52 for moss agate.

ONYX is agate with even, parallel bands usually of black and white or brown and white.

SARDONYX is a form of onyx with alternating bands of sard (carnelian) and white—that is, of red and white bands.

CHERT, or hornstone, is an impure form of flint—usually more brittle. Colour: white, yellow, grey, or brown.

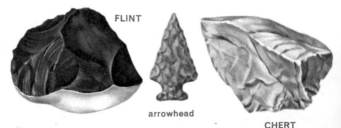

FLINT

arrowhead

CHERT

CARNELIAN

CHRYSOPRASE

ONYX

BANDED AGATE

EYE AGATE

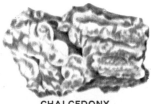

CHALCEDONY

JASPER

COMMON OPAL

HYALITE

GEYSERITE

DIATOMS (magnified)

TRIPOLITE

OPAL is a non-crystalline form of quartz—a silica gem containing varying amounts of water (usually 3 to 9 per cent). Opal forms as a low-temperature deposit around hot springs and in veins. It makes up the skeletons of diatoms and siliceous sponges. Opal is usually colourless or white, with colour only in gem forms. H. 5.5 to 6.5; Sp. Gr. 2.1. Lustre glassy, pearly, or resinous. Streak, white. Among the varieties are:

Common Opal Milky white, green yellow to brick red; somewhat translucent, glassy, or resinous. Widespread, often in volcanic rocks. Various names for different colours and gem forms (p. 86).

Hyalite is a clear, colourless, glassy opal encrusting rocks or filling small veins. Sometimes translucent or white.

Geyserite or siliceous sinter is a form of opal found around geysers and hot springs. It may be firm, porous, or fibrous; usually grey or white, and opaque. Often forms odd structures.

Tripolite is formed of microscopic shells of diatoms (diatomite) and other organisms. White, chalky, fine-grained, but hard. Will scratch glass.

GEM MINERALS

GEMS are the most prized and famous of all minerals. All are better, clearer, or more crystalline forms of minerals which in common occurrences are less beautiful and less spectacular. Diamonds, emeralds, rubies, and sapphires stand out as the true gems. Other stones are classified as semiprecious and ornamental stones. Scarcity and fashion are important in determining the value of a gem, but the following physical properties are prized: lustre, transparency, colour, and hardness.

Lustre depends on how light is reflected by the mineral. The transparent gems also refract or bend light and are cut to turn the light back into the observer's eye. Colour is essential in some gems, and incidental in others. It may add or detract greatly from the gem's value. The harder the gem, the better it resists scratching of its polished surfaces. Here are some of the best-known gems and semiprecious stones. Many other minerals and some rocks are occasionally used as gems.

brown

yellow

green

DIAMONDS are pure carbon (C); H. 10; Sp. Gr. 3.5. Found as isometric crystals or crystalline masses. Colourless or with tints of yellow, pink, blue, brown, and black. When not of gem quality, diamonds have important industrial uses as abrasives.

DIAMOND IN MATRIX

TRANSPARENT GEMS are striking for their lustre and brilliance and often for hardness and colour too. Most are oxides of aluminium, beryllium, and magnesium, sometimes with silica. All quartz gems (pp. 86-87) are silica.

Some transparent gems are identical minerals that differ only in colour, as the ruby and the sapphire. Transparency, lack of flaws, colour, and size determine the value of these gems. For synthetic gems, see pp. 92-93.

AQUAMARINE CRYSTAL

AQUAMARINE is a light blue-green form of beryl ($3BeO \cdot Al_2O_3 \cdot 6SiO_2$), only ore of the metal beryllium. H. 7.5 to 8. It also occurs as yellowish golden beryl.

CHRYSOBERYL

CHRYSOBERYL differs from beryl in being $BeO \cdot Al_2O_3$. Hardness 8.5; Sp. Gr. 3.6. Colour: green, possibly due to chromium. Alexandrite, a dark green form, is red by transmitted light.

EMERALD

EMERALD is a form of beryl varying in colour from light to deep emerald green. Oriental emerald, a green corundum gem, is harder and may be the most valuable gem.

RUBY CRYSTAL

"brilliant" cut ruby

CORUNDUM MINERALS are all rare forms of alumina (Al_2O_3). The gems vary in colour. Deep red rubies are valued more than diamonds. Star sapphires reflect light in a six-pointed star, as do a few other minerals. Green, purple, and yellow corundum are known as oriental emerald, oriental amethyst, and oriental topaz.

STAR SAPPHIRE

cut sapphire

TOPAZ, a mineral of granites and other igneous rocks, is an alumino-fluoro-silicate. Large crystals have been found, some of gem quality. These are usually yellow, brown, or pink (when heated). H. 8; Sp. Gr. 3.5. False topaz is brownish quartz.

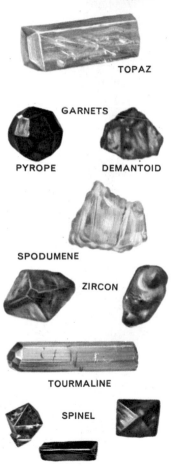

TOPAZ

GARNETS are a common group of silicate minerals (pp. 104-105), sometimes of gem quality. Pyrope and almandite are best known. Green demantoid is also a gem.

GARNETS

PYROPE   DEMANTOID

SPODUMENE ($LiAlSi_2O_6$) occurs in pegmatite rocks, often forming long crystals. Two gem forms exist: Hiddenite, a green gem spodumene from North Carolina, and kunzite, pink coloured, first found near San Diego, Cal. Gem spodumenes also occur in Brazil.

SPODUMENE

ZIRCON ($ZrSiO_4$) is common in igneous rocks, but fairly rare as a gem stone. Clear brown crystals turn blue when heated and hence make better gems.

ZIRCON

TOURMALINE, commonly black (p. 95), forms long crystals, sometimes varicoloured. Red, green, brown, and blue tourmalines are known.

TOURMALINE

SPINEL ($MgAl_2O_4$) sometimes reaches gem quality, the best red gems coming from Ceylon. Brown, green, and even blue spinels occur. H. 8; Sp. Gr. 3.8.

SPINEL

85

QUARTZ GEMS, the best known semiprecious stones, are the same as the minerals described on pp. 76-82. Of these gems, opals are the most valuable, some being classified as precious. The transparent quartz gems range from colourless through yellow, brown, blue, black,

ASTERIATED ROSE QUARTZ

CITRINE

SMOKY QUARTZ

AMETHYST

THREE CUTS OF ROCK CRYSTAL

PRECIOUS OPAL

FIRE OPAL

BLACK OPAL

purple, pink and, rarely, green. The translucent or opaque quartz gems have an even wider array of colours and forms. Some are banded, striped, or mottled. Names of all these gems vary locally. Some bear several names; some names are used for several stones.

WHITE CHALCEDONY

AGATE

SARD

ONYX

JASPER

BLOODSTONE

CHRYSOPRASE

CARNELIAN

CARVED JADE

JADE is the name given a group of opaque, waxy or pearly minerals, usually green but also yellow, white, or pink. There are two kinds of "true jade". One is jade-ite, a gem form of pyroxene. The other is nephrite, a form of amphibole (pp. 100-101). Light, translucent, emerald green jade-ite is considered a precious stone.

MOONSTONE is albite (p. 99) with a bluish sheen.

AMAZONITE is a green form of gem-quality microcline (p. 99).

LAPIS-LAZULI is a rock rich in lazurite. Usually an ornamental stone, it is also used as a gem.

MALACHITE, often with azurite (pp. 32-33), occurs in masses. Cut for gems or ornaments.

OPAQUE GEMS, with the exception of jade, grade off into ornamental stones. The group includes representatives of metallic ores and rock-forming minerals. Some, like obsidian, lapis, and jet, are better classified as rocks. One unusual mineral that could fit in this group is the

RHODONITE may be used as a gem stone because of its colour and hardness. See also pp. 52-53.

RHODOCHROSITE, softer than rhodonite, has the same attractive pink colour. See also pp. 52-53.

HEMATITE, an iron mineral (pp. 40-42), is cut as a black, shiny gem when crystalline.

JET, a tough form of soft coal, takes a high polish. A semiprecious gem from England and Spain.

OBSIDIAN or volcanic glass (p. 116) has long been used for arrowheads and primitive cutting tools. It polishes well and makes an attractive semiprecious stone.

TURQUOISE, a copper-and-aluminium phosphate mineral, is prized by western Indians. Good quality turquoise is rare. Cheap stones are often dyed blue.

pearl, formed by a number of fresh-water and marine molluscs when sand or some other material irritates the animal's mantle. Layers of aragonite form the pearl, which grows year by year. Pearls are soft (H. 4), but have a unique lustre.

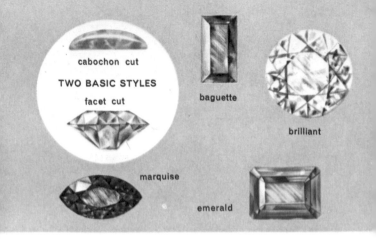

cabochon cut

TWO BASIC STYLES

facet cut

baguette

brilliant

marquise

emerald

THE CUTTING OF PRECIOUS STONES is done
with the object of bringing out their qualities. The rounded forms (cabochon) produced by merely polishing—
formerly the only forms known—are no longer used
except for the softer, opaque stones such as opal and
turquoise.

Cutting transparent gems into facets ensures the max-
imum play of light, i.e. the brilliancy. The relative incli-
nation of the facets causes multiple internal and external reflections. The work of the lapidary, the art of
cutting precious stones, was not fully developed till the
15th century. It requires great patience and exceptional
skill, particularly when working on diamonds, whose
extreme hardness makes the stone resistant to any other
material.

The rough stone is first of all examined to determine
the lines of cleavage, knowledge of which saves both
time and material. After cleaning, the stone is cemented

to the end of a stick or handle, so that it can be held firmly. It is then divided along a line of cleavage by being given sharp taps with a pointed hammer. Or it may be sawn by the action, through many hours or even days, of a phosphor-bronze disc rotating at high speed. Next, the rough cutting or "brutage" is done with diamond powder applied by a mill. With the stone now roughly symmetrical, the facets are cut by grinding one stone against another. Further facets can be added in the polishing, also done by a mill, the chief object of which is to remove the last imperfections. To remove all traces of diamond dust or oil, the stone is finally boiled in sulphuric acid.

The cutting of other gems is rendered much easier by their being softer. Splinters from the cuttings of the harder stones are used in jewellery or in precision machinery (diamonds and rubies).

The unit of weight for precious stones is the carat, which is about 3½ grains. The largest of all diamonds, the Cullinan, was found in 1905. In its rough state it weighed 3,106 carats. It was cut into 9 large brilliants and 95 smaller ones. Of the more historic stones the most famous is the Koh-i-noor. It weighed 186 carats when presented to Queen Victoria in 1850, but was later recut and is now 106 carats.

diamond wheel
cutting agate

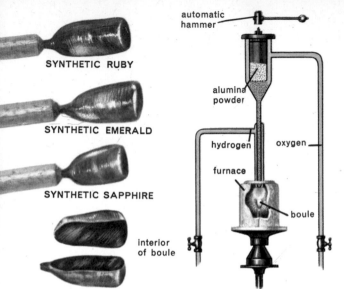

SYNTHETIC RUBY

SYNTHETIC EMERALD

SYNTHETIC SAPPHIRE

interior of boule

automatic hammer

alumina powder

hydrogen

oxygen

furnace

boule

SYNTHETIC GEMS—once a dream—during the past few decades have become a reality. Besides the economic problems there were ample scientific ones. Attempts to make synthetic diamonds about the turn of the century met with dubious success. The problem seems to have been solved by renewed efforts in 1955. The goal here was to produce industrial diamonds, rather than gems. In this direction, a new synthetic, borazon, produced in 1957 seems to be as hard as diamond and much better able to withstand high temperatures. It is with corundum, however, that the best synthetic gems have been made. A method of fusing fine alumina (Al_2O_3) in a very hot flame was perfected in 1902. By adding the appropriate mineral pigments, synthetic rubies, sapphires, emeralds, and similar gems of large size and fine quality have been formed.

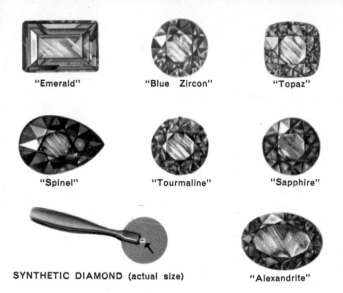

"Emerald"

"Blue Zircon"

"Topaz"

"Spinel"

"Tourmaline"

"Sapphire"

SYNTHETIC DIAMOND (actual size)

"Alexandrite"

In the apparatus shown on p. 92, the alumina mixture sifts down through the oxyhydrogen flame and forms a slow-growing *boule* at the end of the ceramic rod. Synthetic jewels are universally used for watches, and it is hard to tell synthetic corundum gems from natural ones.

Besides the corundum gems, a number of other synthetic gems have been produced. These are chemically identical to the natural gems. Other man-made gems are without natural counterparts and, finally, there are imitations made of glass. Gems may also be dyed (as agates) or have their colour changed by heat, chemical action, or radioactivity. A thin layer of precious stone is sometimes mounted on a larger backing of inexpensive material (p. 15). For these and other reasons it is wise to get expert help when selecting valuable stones.

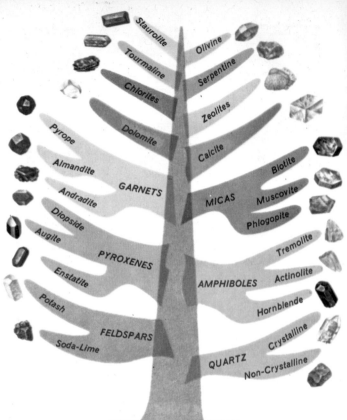

ROCK-FORMING MINERALS

The minerals on this tree are the ones that are of major importance in forming the rocks of the earth's crust. Some rocks have no definite minerals—just organic or glassy material. But most of them do contain discrete minerals—those from the groups pictured above predominating.

ROCK-FORMING MINERALS

ROCK-FORMING MINERALS are as miscellaneous a group as the gems. They are important as the building blocks of the solid earth, from which mountains are made and valleys carved. They furnish the minerals of our soil and the salt of the seas. Most of these minerals contain metals, but they are not metallic ores. Some are valued as gems when, under rare circumstances, they attain gem quality. A few are of commercial value, but it is as basic constituents of rocks (p. 109) that the true value of the group is realized.

Nearly all the rock-forming minerals are silicates, that is, they consist of a metal combined with silicon and oxygen. Some are complex silicates, involving several metals and several silicate groups. This complexity makes chemical testing of rock-forming minerals a difficult matter. But the common minerals of igneous and metamorphic rocks can be identified by paying close attention to their physical properties.

In the rock-forming group are some minerals treated elsewhere. Quartz (pp. 76-82), especially in its crystalline forms, is very common in rocks. Calcite and dolomite (pp. 63-65) can also be called rock-forming minerals; so can halite and gypsum.

BLACK TOURMALINE

TOURMALINE, a silicate of aluminium with boron and several other metals, is occasionally abundant with mica and feldspars in granitic rocks. It is mostly black—other colours forming gems (p. 85). Note the triangular, striated crystals. H. 7; Sp. Gr. 3.

MICAS are an unusual family of minerals, famous because of the perfect basal cleavage which enables one to cleave off paper-thin, flexible sheets. Such sheets from large "books" made the heatproof windows of old stoves and ranges. Because of their high electrical resistance, the iron-free micas are widely used in many kinds of electrical and electronic equipment. This important use has led to the experimental production of artificial micas.

Micas are silicate minerals. All include oxides of aluminium and silicon with other metals, singly or in combination. They also contain some water in combination with the other elements. Part of this water (about 5 per cent) is lost when micas are heated. Micas are common in granites and similar igneous rocks. Large, six-sided crystals—some weighing as much as 100 lbs.—occur in pegmatites. The best and most perfect "books" are from large deposits in India.

Micas also form in metamorphic rocks as other minerals are altered by heat and pressure. The mica in mica schist and in gneiss is of this origin, as is the mica in some kinds of crystalline marble.

as found—

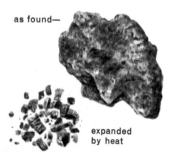

expanded
by heat

VERMICULITES are clay minerals containing water, closely related to the micas. When they are heated, steam forms and practically explodes the flaky mineral, expanding it to many times its original volume. A soft yellow or bronze material, it is used for insulation and for lightweight aggregates. It is excellent for growing cuttings and seedlings.

BIOTITE is a dark-coloured mica, brown or black, sometimes green, containing magnesium and iron. It is abundant in some granites and is also common in schists and gneiss. Small barrel-shaped crystals are sometimes found. Biotite may occur with muscovite in metamorphic rocks. Thin cleavage sheets often show light spots, rings, or halos. H. 2.5-3; Sp. Gr. 2.9.

MUSCOVITE is a pale, almost colourless mica—H. 2.2; Sp. Gr. 2.8. It is a potash mica of variable chemical composition. Named after Muscovy, where it was used as a substitute for glass, this common mica occurs in many places. Crystals are common and may include flattened garnets, quartz, or tourmaline. Abundant in granites and pegmatites.

PHLOGOPITE, related to biotite and found with it, is a magnesium-potassium mica often containing iron and fluorine. Hardness and specific gravity much like muscovite. Large crystals of phlogopite are mined in Ontario and Madagascar. It is the mica usually seen as brown flecks in crystalline dolomite and marble.

LEPIDOLITE is a lithium mica with potassium and fluorine, also quite variable in composition. It is an ore of the light metal lithium. Some deposits occur in New England; more near San Diego, Cal., where one finds both an attractive lavender and a pale yellow form. Lepidolite gives a crimson flame colour.

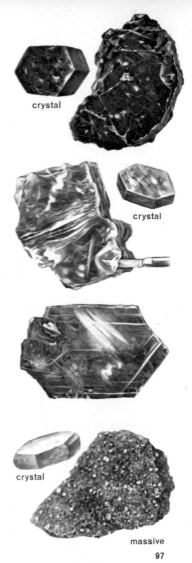

crystal

crystal

crystal

massive

97

LABRADORITE — an iridescent blue plagioclase feldspar used in ornament and decoration.

FELDSPARS form the most abundant group of minerals. If the group were considered a single mineral (and there is good reason for this), it would be the most common mineral by far—five times as common as quartz. Feldspars are found in nearly all igneous rocks and in rocks formed from them. All are aluminium silicates combined with one or two more metals. Feldspars have common physical properties. Their crystal forms are very similar and the crystal angles are all close to 60° and 120°. Feldspars show two good cleavage faces, at right angles or nearly so. Their hardness is 6 or a bit more, and their specific gravity about 2.6. They usually have a smooth, glassy, or pearly lustre.

Feldspars may be classified by crystal structure or by chemical composition. Neither is of much help to the amateur. From the chemical point of view, the potash feldspars (orthoclase and microcline) are put in one group. The other group, containing the plagioclase feldspars, begins with albite (a sodium feldspar) and ends with anorthite (a calcium feldspar). Between these are feldspars that are difficult to identify because they contain varying proportions of sodium and calcium, as oligoclase, andesine, and labradorite. Rarer feldspars with barium and other metals are also known to occur.

Feldspars are widely used in ceramic industries in the manufacture of glazes, flux enamels, and binders. They ultimately decay to form kaolin (p. 49) or other clay minerals (p. 150).

ORTHOCLASE, a fairly common feldspar, is usually white, yellow, or pink. It is a potash feldspar, some varieties containing sodium; in others barium may replace the potassium. A variety known as adularia, with a bluish reflected sheen, is sometimes cut as moonstone, a semiprecious stone. Another variety, sanidine, is found in volcanic rock.

MICROCLINE is also a potash feldspar—the most common one. Both it and orthoclase lack the fine lines or striations seen on the cleavage faces of plagioclase feldspars. Microcline is also found in a pale green colour (amazonite, p. 88), sometimes of gem quality. The best crystals are from granite.

ALBITE is one of the plagioclase feldspars. It is a sodium feldspar with a slightly lower specific gravity than others, and frequently contains potassium. The basal cleavage surface is marked with fine lines. Colour white, grey, or bluish, often with a bluish sheen. Some are cut as moonstones. Albite is common in granitic rocks and in acidic lavas.

ANORTHITE is a calcium felspar which ends the series beginning with albite. Between them is oligoclase, with 15 to 25 per cent calcium. Oligoclase is common in granites. Anorthite is less common; it occurs in several forms, mainly white, grey or glassy. Small amounts of sodium are usually present.

crystal

Albite twinning

ACTINOLITE—green; fibrous or radiating, glassy crystals.

HORNBLENDE H. 5 to 6; Sp. Gr. 3 to 3.4. Crystals common.

TREMOLITE—white, grey, or colourless; usually long, bladed crystals.

AMPHIBOLES are complex hydrous silicates containing calcium, magnesium, and iron. Crystals are often long or needle-like; sometimes fibrous (p. 75). When short, they are six-sided. The cleavage planes are at about 55° and 125°, forming wedge-shaped cleavage fragments. These characteristics are important in separating amphiboles from pyroxenes (p. 101). Hornblende, dark green to black and glassy, is found in basic igneous rocks and in such altered rocks as hornblende schist. It contains aluminium and is most often of secondary origin.

Actinolite and tremolite may be considered one mineral or two. The crystal forms are the same but in actinolite some of the magnesium is replaced by iron, giving the mineral a green colour. Both are secondary minerals related to amphibole jades and asbestos (p. 75).

ENSTATITE H. 5.5; Sp. Gr. 3.5. Colour variable.

crystal

crystals

AUGITE H. 5 to 6; Sp. Gr. 3.5. Green to black; glassy.

DIOPSIDE H. 5 to 6; Sp. Gr. 3.4. Colour white to green and brown — sometimes transparent.

PYROXENES are complex silicates, closely related to the amphiboles. Pyroxenes are often found as primary minerals in igneous rocks. Their cleavage angles are close to 90°, giving squared cleavage fragments. They too are often fibrous or needle-like. Most are grey or green, grading into black. The kinds of pyroxenes are not distinct. They vary chemically as iron replaces calcium and magnesium. When this occurs, enstatite becomes hypersthene and diopside becomes hedenbergite. Enstatite is sometimes found in meteorites from outer space. Diopside, usually a light green, is most common in metamorphosed dolomitic marbles. Augite, the most common pyroxene, is a complex of aluminium, magnesium, calcium, and iron silicates found in nearly all basic igneous rocks and dark lavas, dikes, and sills.

ZEOLITES are not major rock formers but they are widely distributed. All are chemically related to the feldspars —with the addition of water, chemically combined. This water is held loosely, so all zeolites boil and bubble when heated by a blowpipe. Their name means "boiling stone". About 25 minerals fit into the zeolite group. In addition there are several zeolite associates—minerals chemically similar but not of the zeolite pattern. Zeolites and their associates are often found in lavas, filling cavities and veins. All are pale, fairly soft minerals of low density. The ability of zeolites to interchange ions of calcium and sodium has promoted the manufacture of artificial zeolites for use as water softeners.

Stilbite often occurs in pearly, sheaf-like masses of twinned crystals. Radiating crystals, often translucent, may also form rounded knobs. Colour: white, yellow, to reddish-brown. H. 3.5 to 4; Sp. Gr. 2.1.

Chabazite occurs with stilbite, usually in the form of large rhombohedral—almost cubic—crystals. It is white, occasionally pink, with a glassy lustre; transparent or translucent. H. 4 to 5; Sp. Gr. 2.1.

Natrolite forms slender, prismatic needle-like crystals. It fuses in the heat of a candle flame—a distinguishing characteristic. Colour, white to yellowish. H. 5; Sp. Gr. 2.2; lustre, glassy.

Pectolite is seen in tapering masses of thin needles sometimes several inches long. H. 5; Sp. Gr. 2.8. Colour usually white; lustre silky. It is also fibrous or may form radiating masses. Pectolite needles are dangerously sharp and should be handled with care.

Prehnite and pectolite are zeolite associates which may occur together. Prehnite is usually in compact masses of flat light-green crystals. Lustre, glassy; brittle and translucent. H. 6 to 6.5; Sp. Gr. 2.9.

STILBITE

CHABAZITE

NATROLITE

PECTOLITE

PREHNITE

GARNETS are better known as gems than as rock-forming minerals, but they are common and form a small but conspicuous ingredient of igneous and metamorphic rocks. Garnets are a close-knit family of silicate minerals with many common characteristics. They all form crystals in the isometric system, usually with 12 or 24 sides, though sometimes combined forms with 36 or 48 faces are found.

Chemically, garnets contain the elements calcium, magnesium, iron, and aluminium, combined with silicon and oxygen. Other, less common metals may also occur.

in phyllite

GROSSULARITE is a calcium-aluminium garnet, normally colourless to white, but colored when it contains iron as an impurity. It is found mainly in marble. A warm-brown variety from Ceylon is cut as a gem. The name refers to a Siberian "gooseberry green" variety.

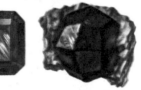

cut gem   crystal

PYROPE is sometimes called precious garnet, though it is mined in large quantities for garnet paper. Clear, perfect specimens are found in South African "blue earth" with diamonds; they make fine gems. Pyrope is a magnesium-aluminium garnet.

Crystals in mica schist

ALMANDITE is the "common garnet" found in many metamorphic rocks. It is an iron-aluminium garnet, though part of the iron may be replaced by magnesium—making such forms similar to pyrope. When it has a clear red colour it is sometimes—like pyrope—called precious garnet and is cut as a gem.

Crystals are abundant—from pinhead size up to 4 in. in diameter. Fresh crystals have a glassy lustre. There is no distinct cleavage. All garnets have a hardness of about 7. Their density is more variable, between 3.4 and 4.3—depending on the metals in them. Most garnets are found in schists, gneiss, and marbles. Some occur in lavas and in granites.

Only a small percentage of garnets are of gem quality. In a few large deposits, garnets are mined and crushed for garnet paper and other abrasives.

SPESSARTITE is quite a rare member of the group of aluminium garnets. It contains manganese and aluminium. The manganese often gives the garnet a violet tint which makes gem-quality specimens particularly valuable.

crystal in schist

ANDRADITE is a garnet containing calcium and iron. It, too, is very common and like almandite is called common garnet. Colour varies from yellow to green, red, and black, depending on impurities. It occurs in igneous rocks and in some metamorphosed limestones. The green form, demantoid, is a gem (p. 85).

UVAROVITE is a less common garnet found in serpentine rock and in limestones associated with chromium ores. It is a calcium-chromium garnet. The chromium gives it its rich green colour. It is unlike most garnets in that a splinter of it will not fuse when heated with a blowpipe.

OLIVINE

OLIVINE, also called chrysolite or peridot, is the most common member of a group of silicates. Olivine is a magnesium-iron silicate, coloured various shades of green (rarely, brown); H. 6.5 to 7; Sp. Gr. 3.3. Lustre, glassy; transparent to translucent. Clear varieties are cut as the gem peridot. Olivine is found in igneous rocks that are rich in magnesium and low in quartz, as basalt and gabbro; also in metamorphosed dolomites. It is often found in the form of small grains or in large, granular masses. The crystals are relatively rare, though occasionally some have been found up to several inches long.

CHLORITE is one, two, three, or more minerals depending on how carefully the constituents are separated. If considered a single mineral, chlorite is a mixture of magnesium and iron-aluminium silicates, with water. It often forms as an alteration of rocks rich in pyroxenes, amphiboles, and biotite. It may also form in cavities of

basic igneous rocks. Chlorite is usually green but may vary from white to brown and black. H. 2 to 2.5; Sp. Gr. 2.8; pearly lustre; streak, greenish or white. It forms in masses, crusts, fibres, or bladed crystals. The crystals have a perfect basal cleavage and, like mica, split into thin sheets. These may bend slightly, like selenite, but are not elastic like mica.

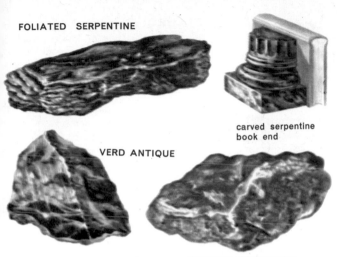

FOLIATED SERPENTINE

carved serpentine
book end

VERD ANTIQUE

COMMON SERPENTINE

SERPENTINE (chemically similar to chlorite) is a magnesium silicate with water, but may include small amounts of iron or nickel. The fibrous form of serpentine, chrysotile asbestos, is described on p. 75. A number of other varieties depend on physical characteristics, especially colour and lustre. Common or massive serpentine ($H_4Mg_3Si_2O_9$) varies from cream white through all shades of green to black. Streak is white. H. 2.5 to 4; Sp. Gr. 2.6; translucent to opaque. Note the greasy or waxy lustre and feel of serpentine. Some weathered specimens are earthy. There are micaceous, fibrous, and mottled varieties, some of them fluorescent.

The mineral serpentine is a secondary mineral which also occurs as metamorphosed serpentine rock. Deposits are large but at present have only minor use in firebricks. Serpentine marble (verd antique) and deeply coloured common serpentine are used for carvings.

twinned crystals

STAUROLITE is an iron-aluminium silicate often found with garnets in such metamorphic rocks as schists, phyllites, and gneisses. Brown to black in colour; streak, grey; H. 7 to 7.5; Sp. Gr. 3.7. Staurolite almost always occurs in crystals—as orthorhombic prisms and commonly as twinned crystals. Twinning may be at 60° or 90°. When at 90°, the twin crystals form a perfect cross. Such crystals (fairy crosses), broken or weathered from the bedrock, are sold as charms or souvenirs. These may be up to 2 in. long, but are usually an inch or less. Transparent crystals occur rarely, and may be cut as gems.

EPIDOTE is one of a group of complex silicates of calcium and aluminium with water. It forms in nearly every type of metamorphic rock, in cracks and seams, as crystals or as thin green crusts. It is a typical mineral where igneous rocks have come in contact with limestones. Crystals are usually slender prisms, grading into needle-like forms. Colour, green to brown and black; H. 6 to 7; Sp. Gr. 3.3. Easily identified by hardness and colour.

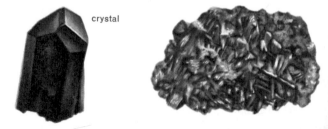

crystal

massive

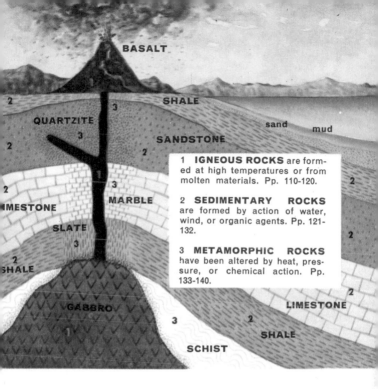

Within the illustration:

BASALT

2   3   SHALE

QUARTZITE   3   SANDSTONE   sand   mud

2   2

2   1   3   MARBLE   2

LIMESTONE   SLATE   2

2   3   2

SHALE

GABBRO   1   3   2   LIMESTONE   2

SHALE

SCHIST

1 **IGNEOUS ROCKS** are formed at high temperatures or from molten materials. Pp. 110-120.

2 **SEDIMENTARY ROCKS** are formed by action of water, wind, or organic agents. Pp. 121-132.

3 **METAMORPHIC ROCKS** have been altered by heat, pressure, or chemical action. Pp. 133-140.

ROCKS

Rocks are large masses of material that make up the earth's crust. Some do not have discrete minerals but are composed of glasses or of organic materials like coal. Many rocks are not solid—as soil, gravel, sand, and clay. A rock may consist of a single mineral, as quartz, gypsum, or dolomite. Most rocks contain several minerals, or were formed from older rocks in which these minerals were present.

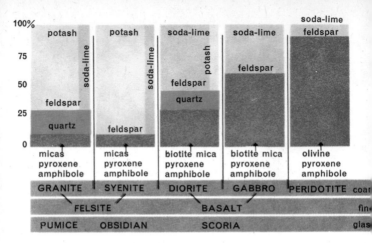

IGNEOUS ROCKS

Igneous rocks are classified by their texture, mineral content, and origin. They all come from magmas—molten mixture of minerals, often rich in gases, found deep below the surface. If magmas cool beneath the surface they form *intrusive* rocks and develop typical structures that may later be exposed by erosion. Magmas reaching the surface form *extrusive* rocks, such as the spectacular volcanic rocks.

Igneous rocks usually contain ferro-magnesian minerals (amphiboles, pyroxenes, micas, or olivine) and feldspar or feldspar-like minerals. Many contain quartz. Those rich in light minerals (quartz and potash feldspar) are called acidic. These are light not only in colour but in weight (average Sp. Gr. 2.6 to 2.7). Those richer in ferromagnesian minerals are called basic. They are darker and heavier (Sp. Gr. 3.0 and more). In texture, igneous rocks range from those with large crystals to glassy rocks with no crystals at all.

INTRUSIVE ROCKS form as magmas cool. This is a gradual process in which the more volatile chemicals remain as liquids and gases longer. Some intrusive rocks, very near the surface, grade into extrusive types. Those that cool deeper are more coarsely crystalline.

Granite is the best known of the deeper igneous (plutonic) rocks. It is usually light-coloured, formed mainly of potash feldspar (about 60 per cent) and quartz (about 30 per cent), usually with mica or hornblende. The intergrown mineral crystals are all about the same size—a characteristic of slow cooling. Fine granite has a salt-and-pepper pattern. Feldspar may redden it. Granite is hard and tough, widely used in construction and monuments. Some granites may be metamorphic rocks (p. 140).

MEDIUM-GRAINED GRANITE

quartz

feldspar

biotite mica

FINE-GRAINED GRANITE

RED GRANITE

OTHER INTRUSIVE ROCKS include some which have cooled near the surface. These may contain a groundmass of crystalline grains surrounding larger crystals. Such igneous rocks made of crystals (phenocrysts) in a finer groundmass are known as porphyries.

PEGMATITE is a coarse-grained vein or dike rock with crystals that range from an inch or so to many feet in length. Pegmatites are mined for their mica and feldspar, or for gems and other accessory minerals. They often contain cavities or vugs lined with crystals. In one form, graphic granite, the quartz forms angular figures which look like writing.

Some accessory pegmatite minerals:

garnet	arsenopyrite	spodumene
apatite	tourmaline	emerald
topaz	lepidolite	cryolite
beryl	chrysoberyl	sapphire
ruby	molybdenite	rubellite
pyrite	aquamarine	wolframite
fluorite	cassiterite	uraninite

SYENITE is less common than granite. It lacks quartz entirely or may have a small amount, in which case it is known as quartz-syenite. Syenite is mainly potash feldspars with some mica or hornblende. The crystals are usually small and the rock is even-textured. Syenite also forms porphyries with phenocrysts of feldspar.

GRANITE PORPHYRY, which forms under somewhat different conditions from granite, has a granite groundmass in which phenocrysts of feldspar, quartz, or biotite mica are embedded. A porphyry is named after the matrix or groundmass—such as syenite porphyry, basalt porphyry. They also occur in extrusive rocks (p. 116).

Porphyries are found in intrusive rocks formed near the surface, and in extrusive rocks, but do not occur in deep-seated intrusives. Pegmatite, granite, and syenite are light-coloured intrusives. Diorite, gabbro, and peridotite are dark, with more ferro-magnesian minerals.

DIORITE is a basic rock rich in minerals such as amphiboles, biotite, or pyroxenes. Its texture is like that of granite, but it is composed mainly of plagioclase feldspar and ferro-magnesian minerals. Other feldspars may be present, and sometimes a bit of quartz. Its colour is usually grey or dull green. Granites grade into diorites through intermediate forms—the granodiorites.

GABBRO, like diorite, has a granitic texture. Since texture depends upon rate of cooling, rocks of gabbro composition vary from fine-grained (diabase) on the outside of a dike or sill (p. 115) to a typical gabbro within. Gabbro is made mainly of plagioclase feldspar and pyroxene, with some olivine, traces of ilmenite, but no quartz. A dark rock, its mineral crystals are deeply intermeshed, making it a very tough rock. Porphyritic gabbros are rare.

Dolerite (or diabase) is the fine-grained gabbro which often occurs in sills or dikes. It grades into basalt at the edges, where it has cooled more rapidly.

PERIDOTITE is a dark, heavy intrusive rock composed mainly of olivine with pyroxene and tiny flecks of phlogopite mica or hornblende. Little or no feldspar is present. Fresh rock is nearly black, but the more common weathered specimens are greenish and softer. Peridotite alters serpentine. The South African diamond deposits occur in peridotite, which, in other places, contains important deposits of nickel, chromium and platinum.

INTRUSIVE ROCK STRUCTURES are the natural forms taken by intrusive rocks. Sometimes these structures form deep beneath the surface. With the passing of time, they may later be exposed as covering rocks are removed by water, ice, or wind. When intrusive structures appear at the surface they may become spectacular features of the landscape. As they weather they produce typical kinds of soil. Rich ore deposits formed with their intrusion may then become available.

BATHOLITHS, the largest intrusions, may cover 100,000 square miles. In the Rockies and Sierra Nevada batholiths are exposed in the mountain cores. Though some are ancient, some are new, indicating that they are part of the continual building up of the earth's crust. As magma wells up it may dissolve some of the surrounding rock. It may spread unevenly, trapping islands of older rock. Batholiths generally contain coarse-grained rocks. They are deeply buried and may not be uncovered for millions of years. Small batholiths are called stocks.

LACCOLITHS might be likened to blisters within the earth's thin skin of sedimentary rocks. Magma spreads outward between rock layers and raises those above it into a dome that may be a thousand feet or more high and from one to ten miles across. Sedimentary layers lifted by the magma may crack, subjecting them to a more rapid erosion which may eventually expose the igneous core. The edges of resistant upturned sedimentary layers around the laccolith may form circular ridges called hogbacks.

Intrusive structures originate from deep reservoirs of magma whose origins are still not clear. Magmas are capable of producing both acidic and basic rocks. Acidic rocks tend to form major structures—batholiths, the cores of mountain ranges, and the great continental shields. Basic rocks occur more frequently in dykes and sills, often grading into extrusive rocks. All extrusive rocks, at one place or another, grade or join into intrusives. Recognizing such structures enables one to interpret the landscape.

DYKES are sheet-like intrusions rising from a batholith (p. 114) or from some other source of magma. These sheets may vary in thickness from a few inches to hundreds of feet, and may extend from a few feet to many miles. The magma forming the dyke follows cracks and joints below the surface, hence dykes characteristically cut across the rock structures. Magma cools rapidly in contact with the surrounding rock. Hence the dyke may differ in texture and composition in these contact zones. The heart of the injected material may metamorphose the adjoining rock (p. 139). Igneous dykes cut the coal measures in many Scottish coalfields, and may be seen in coastal and quarry sections.

SILLS are similar in origin to dykes. While dykes cut across the existing rocks, sills form parallel to them, frequently shouldering their way in between layers of sedimentary rocks. If these layers are tilted, the sill will be tilted also. The Palisades along the Hudson River near New York is a tilted sill of diabase and gabbro. Sills and dykes may occur near volcanoes when lava fills up cracks in previous lava flows

EXTRUSIVE ROCKS embrace a large group, the most common member of which is lava. This molten material pours out through fissures and volcanoes. It spreads in great lava flows or builds up cones. Volcanic explosions throw fragments into the air as volcanic ash or volcanic bombs. The forms and structures of these rocks are

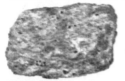

RHYOLITE

RHYOLITE is a light-coloured acidic rock which has very much the same chemical composition as granite. Its texture is very fine. When minerals can be seen in it— phenocrysts of quartz and a glassy feldspar (sanidine)—the rock is a rhyolite porphyry. Colour white to pink to grey, though often reddish from iron stains.

OBSIDIAN

OBSIDIAN and **PUMICE** are chemically the same as rhyolite. Obsidian or natural glass is formed when rhyolitic lava is quickly chilled. Though it is dark-coloured, thin fragments are light and transparent. Indians made knives, arrowheads, and ornaments from this unusual rock. Pitchstone is a duller, rougher form of obsidian. Rhyolite lava blown to a sponge-like consistency by the release of gases forms pumice—a volcanic froth. Pumice is so light it floats on water, and fragments may be washed ashore far from the volcano.

PUMICE

ANDESITE is named after the Andes Mountains, where it is abundant. It contains little or no quartz, and has a greater proportion of ferro-magnesian minerals, which give the rock a darker colour than rhyolite. Porphyries are common, with phenocrysts of feldspar or dark minerals. Andesite is intermediate in composition between rhyolite and basalt. Since rhyolite and andesite are difficult to distinguish in the field, the term felsite is used for both when more accurate identification is impossible.

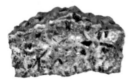

ANDESITE

shown on pp. 118-119. In colour the rocks themselves may be light (acidic) or dark (basic). Like intrusive rocks, the extrusives grade from those rich in quartz to those with no quartz at all. Most of the rocks are fine-grained because of rapid cooling, and are difficult for the amateur to identify and classify.

BASALT is the common dark, heavy lava that is widespread the world over. It is mainly pyroxene and a plagioclase feldspar, but the texture is so fine that these individual minerals are rarely seen. Olivine may also be present. In total, the rock is about half feldspar, half ferro-magnesian minerals. Basalt varies from a dark grey with a greenish tinge to almost black. In arid regions exposed basalt surfaces frequently develop a white, limy encrustation. In humid areas the iron in basalt oxidizes, colouring the surface a rusty brown.

In addition to the dense rock found in lava flows, dykes, and sills, basalt has several other forms. Upper surfaces of basaltic flows may contain gas bubbles which form a porous and cindery rock called scoria. Later the holes or vesicles may become filled with minerals such as calcite, agate, and amethyst, as well as zeolites. When the openings are almond-shaped the name amygdaloidal basalt is used. Large deposits of native copper have been found in such basalts.

arid weathering

humid weathering

BASALT

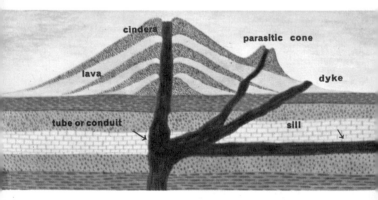

1 cinder cone
2 spatter cone
3 shield lava cone
4 compound volcano
5 radiating dyke

VOLCANOES assume different shapes according to the relative amount of the various materials ejected. Fluid lavas devoid of solid blocks spread readily, forming mountains with gently sloping sides (the Hawaiian type); the more acid lavas, which are also the more viscous, give steeper slopes, or even (as at Mont Pélé) a peak.

cinders

parasitic cone

lava

dyke

tube or conduit

sill

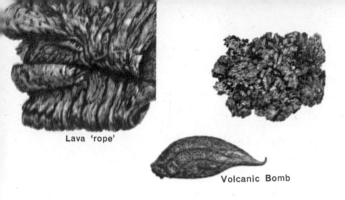

Lava 'rope'

Volcanic Bomb

The ejection of abundant solid matter produces a steep cone of cinders (Strombolian type), sometimes with the crater breached by lava or solid blocks (Vulcanian type).

Most volcanoes are of complex structure, composed of scoriae, cinders, breccia (compacted broken stones), alternating with layers of lava. The slopes of some volcanoes are consolidated by dykes of lava, left in relief by later erosion (Val d'Enfer in the Mont-Dore).

The highly fluid basic lavas produce "fluidal" structures, the cooling lava becoming "ropy". Such outflows, sometimes of great volume, may cover large stretches of land (the Dekkan, Hawaii, Ireland, and the basic plateaux in the Auvergne.)

Pahoehoe is the Hawaiian name for a fluid lava which flows freely and cools with a smooth ropy surface. Such lava flows look like frozen rivers.

Volcanic Bombs are masses of liquid lava thrown into the air. Their motion gives them the elongate shape and smooth surface. Active volcanoes throw vast quantities of gases and steam into the air as well as dust, ashes, and fragments ranging from lapilli (less than 1 in.) to blocks weighing tons.

IGNEOUS ROCKS have long been known to be associated with metal ores. Hot liquids and gases from magmas cool to produce ores directly, or form ores as they react with the local rocks they penetrate. Contact deposits are formed around the edges of batholiths or other large intrusions, especially when these have penetrated into limestones. Veins may extend from igneous masses into the local rock, carrying mineralizing liquids and gases. A system of veins which can be mined as a unit forms a *lode*, like the famous Mother Lode of California gold days. Other veins form as mineralizing solutions penetrate cracks and deposit ores in natural openings or zones of crushed rock.

Most primary ores are sulphides. These and other ores often occur in specific mineral associations. One example is lead-zinc deposits of the Pennines, another the copper and tin association of Cornwall.

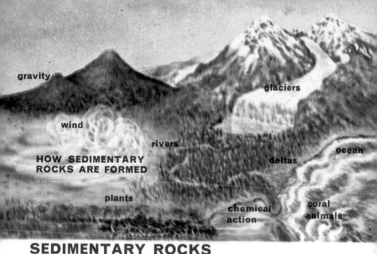

In the image: gravity, wind, glaciers, rivers, ocean, deltas, plants, chemical action, coral animals, and the caption **HOW SEDIMENTARY ROCKS ARE FORMED**

SEDIMENTARY ROCKS

SEDIMENTARY ROCKS are extremely varied, differing widely in texture, colour, and composition. Nearly all are made of materials that have been moved from a place of origin to a new place of deposition. The distance moved may be a few feet or thousands of miles. Running water, wind, waves, currents, ice, and gravity move materials on the surface of the earth by action that takes place only on or very near the surface. In total these rocks cover about three-quarters of the earth's surface.

Unconsolidated mud or sand is usually referred to as a sediment, while consolidated materials are called sedimentary rocks. Rocks made up of grains or particles are called clastic; they may range from less than a thousandth of an inch to huge boulders. Other sedimentary rocks are of chemical or organic origin. Most sedimentary rocks form in layers or strata; many contain fossils. Major sedimentary strata form slowly over millions of years.

Sandstone at Fontainebleau

SANDSTONE is formed by the action of wind, water, and ice on older rock. It is mainly grains of quartz cemented by silica, calcite or iron oxide. Silica cement may produce hard, durable sandstones; the other cements are not as resistant. Sandstones grade off on the coarse side into conglomerates (p. 128) and on the finer side into sandy shales (pp. 124-125). Most sandstones are formed in shallow seas and show signs of near-shore origin—they often include fossil ripple marks and shells of shallow-water animals. In some sandstones, nodules of soft limonite or hematite form "paintpots" once used by Indians.

FALSE-BEDDING IN SANDSTONE. False-bedding may be found where deposits have been formed in relatively shallow water near the mouth of a river (compare the oölitic ore from Lorraine illustrated on p. 126). This peculiar form of stratification is due to successive layers being deposited in different directions.

MEDIUM-GRAINED
SANDSTONE

SANDSTONE
cemented by iron
oxide

ARKOSE—showing
feldspar grains

RIPPLE-MARKS on a piece of sandstone. Many sandstones are formed in shallow water and show ripple-marks, the product of current movement (a familiar sight on sandy beaches) retained as the sandstone solidifies.

CALCAREOUS SHALE   SANDY SHALE

SHALES or mudstones are mainly clays which have hardened into rock. Shales may grade into fine sandstones or, when much is present, into shaly limestones. Since clay particles are exceedingly fine, they tend to be carried into deep or quiet water. Shales are often thin-bedded or laminated, with fairly uniform texture. Their colour is usually grey, but varies from black to dull red.

Clays and shales are frequently so fine-grained that they serve as a barrier to movements of water. Clays and silts that form in lakes may show dark and light alternating layers called *varves*, each pair of layers representing a year's deposit. By counting the varves the age of glacial lakes and other deposits can be estimated. For instance, varve counts indicate that the shales of the Green River formation in Wyoming took over 5 million years to form. Other structures found in shales are shown on the next page. Shales are used in the manufacture of cement. Unconsolidated clays (p. 151) are of tremendous value for ceramic and other uses. Since clays and shales are commonly formed from rocks rich in feldspar, they contain much aluminium silicate. Some shales are oil reservoirs. Milliards of tons of oil shale are a potential source of petroleum for future use—when present high-yield sources will have been depleted.

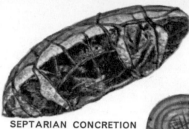

SEPTARIAN CONCRETION
(cross-section)

IRON CONCRETION

CONCRETION

CONCRETIONS are often found in shales, sandstones, and limestones. They may be spherical or flattened masses formed around a fossil or some other nucleus. They may be very small or up to several feet in diameter. Concretions are often harder than the enclosing rock and hence are found as they weather out of it.

MUD CRACKS form as deposits of mud and clay in shallow lakes or on mudflats dry in the sun. The shrinkage forms rough six-sided blocks. Later fresh mud may be washed into the shrinkage cracks. Mud cracks indicate the shallow-water origin of the rock.

consolidated
mud cracks

raindrop imprints in shale

RAINDROPS falling on mud or clay of just the right consistency will leave small pits. Continued rain would wash these away, but a brief shower followed by a period of dryness may preserve raindrop impressions. These are rarer and harder to find than mud cracks.

LIMESTONES are exceedingly variable in colour, texture, and origin. They consist mainly of the mineral calcite (p. 63) and react like calcite chemically. Most of them are of marine origin—some forming at great depths. Both plant and animal life, directly and indirectly, contribute to their formation. Many kinds of animals contribute the minerals that form limestone—corals, worms, crinoids, molluscs, and certain protozoa. Algae are also important lime-precipitating plants. Some limestones are chemical precipitates, while others are cemented fragments of lime.

A unique and complex natural balance is known to involve the carbon-dioxide content of the air, the carbon-dioxide and lime dissolved in the sea, limestone formation, and climatic change. Limestone rocks are a keystone in this structure because they are great reservoirs of carbon dioxide as well as of lime. Since lime is soluble in acid water, limestones dissolve and recrystallize

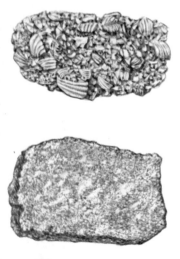

SHELL LIMESTONES include *coquina*, formed recently of shells and fragments loosely cemented. *Chalk* is a limestone made of tiny protozoan shells. Older shell limestones may contain fossil brachiopods, bryozoans, corals, and crinoids. Some of the oldest known sedimentary rocks are limestones formed from algae.

OÖLITIC LIMESTONES usually consist of a mass of small concretions, each built up layer upon layer around some small nucleus. The resulting rock is composed of spherical grains. Oölitic limestones may be formed in shallow water. Each grain grows as it is rolled by waves or currents.

easily. They weather rapidly in humid climates; very slowly in arid ones, where they are good cliff formers—as at Grand Canyon.

Limestones vary from almost unconsolidated masses of shells (such as the kind shown on p. 126) to compact, crystalline rocks. Intimately connected with plant and animal life, they are a rich source of fossils (pp. 130-132). Limestones rich in clay are known as *marls*. They also grade into shales and into sandstones. Some contain silica concretions in the form of chert, flint, or chalcedony (pp. 80-81). A carbonate rock which contains calcium and magnesium carbonate is a dolomitic limestone or a true dolomite (p. 65).

The economic importance of limestones is almost beyond estimation. Limestones are widely used for road metal, in concrete, and for lime. Shaly-limestones are a source of cement. Lead, zinc, fluorite, sulphur, and oil deposits are often associated with limestones.

TUFA is a light, porous limestone often coloured with iron. It forms in springs, where calcite may be deposited on water plants, twigs, or debris. In caves, the secondary deposit of calcium carbonate (*travertine*) forms flowstone, covering walls and floor and sometimes forming stalactites and stalagmites (pp. 63-64).

CRYSTALLINE LIMESTONES form as lime recrystallizes to a greater or lesser extent. These limestones are closely akin to marbles (p. 134) but are considered sedimentary rocks when there is no indication that they have been deformed by pressure. Crystalline limestones used for decoration and ornamentation are sometimes sold as marble.

CONGLOMERATE

CONGLOMERATES are sedimentary rocks composed of rounded pebbles one-fourth of an inch in diameter or larger, cemented in a matrix of finer material. In tillite, a conglomerate of consolidated glacial till, the unassorted fragments may range from gravel size to great boulders. The larger ones may show typical glacial scratches. The coarse materials which form conglomerates are deposited close to shore at the mouths of swift rivers or canyons, in alluvial fans, or in deltas. The pebbles in conglomerates are frequently quartz or quartzite. The cement may be iron oxide, silica, calcium carbonate or, occasionally, clay. Conglomerates grade off into sandstones.

Conglomerates in which the fragments are sharp and angular because they are freshly broken and not worn in transport are called breccias. The various kinds of breccias have little in common other than the angular shape of their components. Some are of volcanic origin, some represent cemented materials in talus slopes or alluvial fans, and some have formed along fault zones. Breccias may be barely consolidated or tightly cemented, depending on their age and on conditions of formation. Commonly they are formed close to the point of origin of the fragments.

QUARTZ BRECCIA
fragments
cemented by silica.

BOG IRON ORE (LIMONITE)

CHEMICALLY FORMED sedimentary rocks are perhaps the most important commercially. Some limestones are precipitated chemically from sea water. Anhydrite, gypsum, and halite (pp. 66-69) form deposits large enough to be considered chemical sedimentary rocks as well as minerals. They are often residues from sea water, which contains about $3\frac{1}{2}$ lbs. of chemical solids in every 100 lbs. of water. Such deposits generally indicate an arid climate at the time of their formation.

Other sedimentary rocks and fuels are formed through biochemical action, and of these coal and oil (pp. 142-145) are the best known. Bacteria may aid in the formation of iron deposits in swamps and shallow lakes, and may be in part responsible for the great Iron Range deposits. Biochemical action may account for the precipitation of manganese also. Diatomaceous earth is a fine deposit of microscopic plant skeletons—forming large, pure deposits of silica.

DIATOMACEOUS EARTH

MODERN DIATOMS
(enlarged)

Arrowheads found buried offer evidence of human life. At left, an ancient folsom point from New Mexico. At right, marine fossils found along Lake Champlain, N. Y., show that this lake was once an arm of the sea.

FOSSILS are the remains, prints, or other indications of former plant or animal life found naturally buried in rock. World-wide studies over the past century indicate that the older the rocks, the simpler the types of plant and animal fossils found in them. The fossils have therefore been used to establish the age of the rock which encloses them. Fossils show that many thousands of kinds of plants and animals, common in the past, no longer exist, and that most of those living today resemble strongly the fossil forms found in relatively recent rocks.

In addition to telling the details of life in the past and the story of such unique animals as giant dinosaurs and titanotheres, fossils also tell of past climates. Colonial corals in Greenland rocks attest to warmer conditions in the past than today, and imprints of fir and spruce in unconsolidated clays near the surface record the penetration of glacial cold far to the south. Fossils are also used to determine the marine or fresh-water origin of rocks.

The occurrence of fossils is both rare and common. Only a tiny fraction of the total number of living things has ever been preserved as fossils, and yet certain layers of rock or strata are made almost entirely of shells, teeth, plant remains, and even of bone.

FOSSILS are preserved in many ways. The simplest is the intact preservation of the hard parts of a plant or an animal, as illustrated on p. 130. Wood, bone, teeth, and other hard parts are preserved intact for relatively short periods.

In another type of fossilization, buried plant or animal materials decompose, leaving a residual film of carbon behind. This may mark the form of a leaf or of some simple animal. On a larger scale this process is responsible for our great deposits of coal.

Sometimes buried material is gradually replaced by silica and other material like calcite, dolomite, or pyrite from solutions which permeate the rock in a process called petrifaction. These replacements form another very common type of fossil.

Probably the most spectacular of all replacements is that of wood by agate or opal as a result of the action of hot, silica-bearing waters. This forms petrified wood. The replacement may be so minute and complete that even the details of cellular structure are preserved. The best-known examples are preserved in the Petrified Forest National Park in Arizona.

CARBONISED FERN LEAF

PETRIFIED WOOD

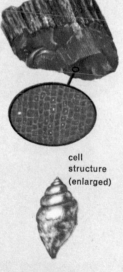

cell
structure
(enlarged)

CAST OF SHELL
in pyrite

131

footstep

impression

cast
mould

cast   mould

BRACHIOPOD

GASTROPOD

MOULDS AND CASTS are very common fossil forms. They are impressions, and so differ from intact preservation and replacements. A footprint, as that of a dinosaur, is a good example of a mould. The impression left in soft mud or silt may harden before more sediment fills it in and provides material for a new layer of rock. If the sediment later consolidates and the rock is eventually broken open, the original imprint will be found below, and filling it will be a cast of the underside of the dinosaur's foot.

When shells are buried in sand or mud, a mould of the outer surface of the shell is formed. Percolating waters may dissolve the shell material completely, and the mould will then be the fossil record. Later, percolating waters may refill the cavity with calcium carbonate or silica, forming a cast which will on its outer surface completely duplicate the external form of the shell.

Palaeontology, the study of plant and animal fossils and their histories, is an important and exciting branch of the science of geology. The study of small fossil forms (which are known as microfossils) has recently yielded a great deal of new information.

METAMORPHIC ROCKS

Metamorphic rocks are rocks which have been changed. Changes may be barely visible, or may be so great that it is impossible to determine what the original rock once was. All kinds of rocks can be metamorphosed—sedimentary, igneous, and other metamorphic rocks. The changes usually bring about a new crystalline structure, the formation of new minerals, and sometimes a coarsening of texture.

Metamorphism results from heat, pressure, or permeation by other substances. Pressure and heat increase with depth in the earth's crust (A, in the illustration above) and may also result from crustal movements (B) or igneous activity (C). Rocks may be permeated by gases or fluids from igneous material (D) or by the percolating of mineral-bearing ground-water.

SIMPLE METAMORPHIC ROCKS is a convenient term applied to rocks formed by the direct alteration of sedimentary rocks where the changes are mainly recrystallization. Few, if any, new minerals are formed. Some of these rocks show parallel structures; others do not.

Slate results from metamorphism of shale, and often traces of the original bedding can be seen. Slate is frequently of a blue-grey colour but may be green, red, or brown. It breaks easily along a flat cleavage plane and can be split into sheets used for roofing or flagstones. Sometimes slate shows folding and wrinkling.

Marbles are recrystallized limestones, normally white, but often tinted by iron oxide, carbon, or serpentine to attractive shades of yellow, brown, green, or black. Limestones and dolomitic limestones may be slightly altered by percolating waters and are often called marbles, but true marbles are the result of metamorphism involving heat and pressure. Secondary minerals may form and crystals may show distortion. Marbles do not often develop the parallel banding and mineral arrangement seen in slates and schists.

Quartzites are usually metamorphosed sandstones which have recrystallized so that, in breaking, they break through the quartz grains instead of through the cement, as in sandstones. The grain structure in quartzite is not nearly so clear as in sandstones. Quartzite, like marble, is a massive metamorphic rock, very hard and tough.

Hornfels are clays or shales which have been metamorphosed through the action of heat from nearby igneous rocks. The hard, recrystallized rock may retain its sedimentary structure, but garnet and other secondary minerals may form. The colour is usually dark; the rock is potted or banded, and may be confused with basalt, especially along contacts.

GREY SLATE

RED SLATE

WHITE MARBLE

BLACK MARBLE

HORNFELS

QUARTZITE

PHYLLITES AND SCHISTS represent the more highly metamorphosed rocks. Phyllite provides the transition, being more metamorphosed than slate but less than schists. Fine grains of mica give it a silky lustre. The schists are coarser than phyllite, with a considerable amount of mica or other secondary minerals. They break in a wavy, uneven surface; this property is called *schistosity*. Schists are named after their most characteristic mineral:

Mica Schist is usually a highly metamorphosed shale composed mainly of many small flakes of mica, oriented roughly parallel, and quartz. Texture varies from fine to coarse, and either staurolite or garnet may be present.

Hornblende Schist is mainly hornblende and quartz. It is dark in colour, and while the minerals have a parallel orientation, hornblende schist does not break cleanly.

Chlorite Schist contains chlorite as a metamorphic mineral instead of mica; this gives it a greenish colour. It has typical schist orientation.

Quartz Schist forms on further metamorphism of impure quartzite. Muscovite mica usually develops as a secondary mineral, and parallel structures also form. Light-coloured.

MINERALS OF METAMORPHIC ROCKS

The following minerals are commonly found in metamorphic rocks

Actinolite	in schists, gneiss and quartzite (p. 100)	**Kyanite**	in schists (p. 48)
Chlorite	in phyllites and schists (p. 106)	**Micas**	muscovite, biotite, and phlogopite in schists, gneiss, and marbles (p. 96)
Diopside	in marbles (p. 101)		
Feldspars	mainly from igneous contacts (p. 98)	**Olivine**	in marbles (p. 106)
Garnets	nearly all kinds— in schists, marble, and phyllites (p. 104)	**Quartz**	in schists, gneiss, and quartzite (p. 76)
		Serpentine and talc	(p. 74) in marbles, soapstones, and schists (pp. 74 and 107)
Graphite	in some schists and marble (p. 62)		
Hornblende	in metamorphosed basic rocks (p. 100)	**Staurolite**	in schists (p. 108)
		Page numbers indicate illustrations.	

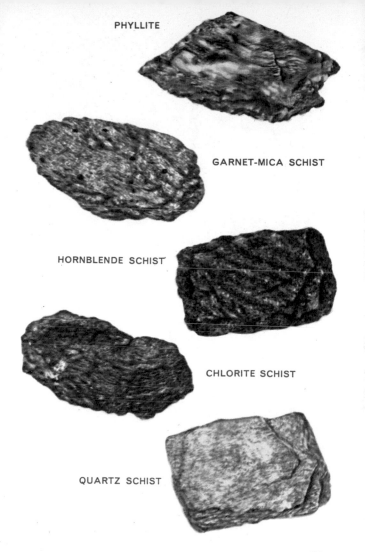

PHYLLITE

GARNET-MICA SCHIST

HORNBLENDE SCHIST

CHLORITE SCHIST

QUARTZ SCHIST

MUSCOVITE GNEISS   GRANITE GNEISS

GNEISS (pronounced nice) may be simply metamorphosed granite, or a far more complex rock with possibly four or five different origins, either igneous or sedimentary. It may also include metamorphic rocks which are invaded by igneous materials so that the rock becomes a complex mixture (migmatite). Schists are often invaded in this way, producing rocks which contain more feldspar and quartz than ordinary schists. The new minerals are often in small lens—like intrusions. Gneiss is hard to define or describe because it is so varied. In general, it is a coarse-textured rock with the minerals in parallel streaks or bands, but lacking schistosity. It is relatively rich in feldspar and usually contains mica or one of the other dark, rock-forming minerals.

Gneiss is classified by its most conspicuous mineral or according to its origin or structures. Characteristics are usually better seen in the field than in hand specimens.

HORNBLENDE GNEISS

INJECTION GNEISS

Muscovite Gneiss is one of the most common kinds, with a pale salt-and-pepper appearance, though biotite mica is common in gneiss also. While the name gives no clue as to the origin, muscovite and biotite gneisses may form from highly metamorphosed, shaly sediments.

Granite Gneiss is named to indicate that it is a metamorphosed granite, though this origin is difficult to establish because of the process of granitization (p. 140). Granite gneiss is rich in feldspars. The mica or hornblende in it is arranged in parallel bands.

Hornblende Gneiss is a dark rock, much darker than biotite gneiss, in which parallel-oriented hornblende replaces mica. It is probably the end result in the metamorphosis of basic igneous rocks.

Injection Gneiss is gneiss which has been permeated by igneous materials during metamorphism. Like schists which are thus altered, it is also known as migmatite.

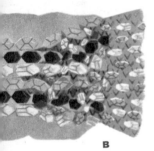

GRANITIZATION is a process in which some form of igneous material or another invades sedimentary or metamorphic rock, producing mixtures which eventually alter the rock so that in texture and composition it becomes like granite. This process may be associated with great batholiths or it may originate with materials coming from an unknown depth in the crust of the earth. The invasion may not even involve gases or liquids as we ordinarily know them. Gradations of rock from granite to gneiss over wide areas is evidence for at least one form of granitization.

One example of the process would be the invasion of gneiss (A) by solutions containing quartz and feldspar that separate the gneiss along parallel bands. In a later stage (B) some parts of the gneiss are transformed while others retain their original structure. As granitization continues, the form and structure of the gneiss minerals change (C), though traces of the parallel arrangement still remain. Finally the original rock is completely absorbed, and the resulting rock shows no traces at all of the gneiss. In structure and composition, it is granite.

WORLD PRODUCTION OF ESSENTIAL MINERALS

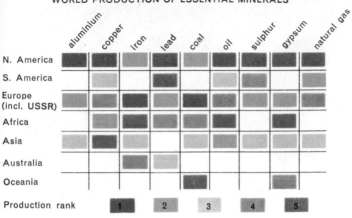

	aluminium	copper	iron	lead	coal	oil	sulphur	gypsum	natural gas
N. America	1	1	3	2	2	1	1	1	1
S. America		3		2		3			4
Europe (incl. USSR)	2	3	1	2	1	2	2	3	2
Africa		2	4		4		2		3
Asia		1	3		3	3		3	3
Australia			2	3					
Oceania					2			2	

Production rank   1   2   3   4   5

ROCKS AND MINERALS
IN DAILY USE

Rocks and minerals are the basis of our civilization. For the life we live today we must have metallic and non-metallic ores, the fuels, and the construction materials such as cements, clays, sand, gravel, and building stones. Then there is the soil, perhaps the most valuable rock of all. Sand, clays, road rock, and soil have a low value per ton compared to metallic ores, but because of the amounts used their overall value is enormous. Since ores have been discussed earlier, this section deals mainly with fuels, soils, and construction materials.

Much of the trouble between nations can be traced to the fact that the rocks, minerals, and fuels are not equally distributed over the earth. Some nations have; others have not. Blood has been shed over gold, silver, iron, coal, oil and uranium. This is still a critical matter for us all.

141

BITUMINOUS

ANTHRACITE

LIGNITE

COAL is the fuel which made the industrial revolution possible. About a milliard and a half tons are still mined annually (200 million tons in the United Kingdom). Coal is an organic sedimentary rock consisting of the altered remains of plants. It is formed by a slow series of changes marked by a loss of water and volatile substances and a corresponding increase in the amount of "fixed carbon". Coal is classified by the relative amount of these three groups of materials. Peat, which contains about 80 per cent moisture, is not considered a form of coal.

Lignite, the lowest rank or kind of coal, has a heating value of 7,400 British Thermal Units (B.T.U.). It is brown in colour and breaks down into powdered or flaky fragments when stored. It burns with a smoky flame.

Bituminous or soft coals are black coals which often have a cubic fracture and a dull lustre. They yield from 9,700 to 15,400 B.T.U. and total 90 per cent of the coal mined. The higher grades of bituminous coal store well and burn with an almost smokeless flame.

Anthracite or hard coal is hard and durable. It stores well and burns with a very short smokeless flame. Anthracite has a conchoidal fracture and a black shiny lustre— sometimes iridescent. It forms when folding or metamorphism drives a larger amount of volatile matter out of soft coal than would otherwise be lost.

Most of the high-grade coals of the world were formed during the Carboniferous period, when a warm climate favoured the rapid growth of fern-like plants. Coals are also found in the Jurassic of Scotland, and there are extensive deposits of lignite in the Tertiary rocks of northern Europe. The coal-bearing rocks are sometimes thousands of feet thick, with layers of coal up to 100 feet thick lying between layers of sandstones and shales. The world's reserves of coal are very roughly estimated at a total of about seven billion tons, of which over half is in North America. Not all of these reserves are usable at the present price of coal.

CHEMICAL COMPOSITION OF COALS

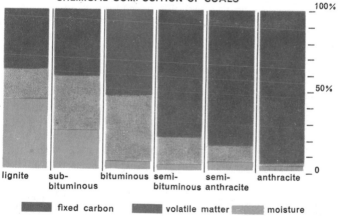

fixed carbon   volatile matter   moisture

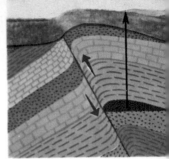
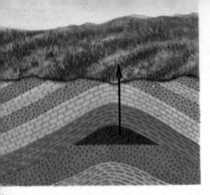

ANTICLINES or upward folds provide traps for oil and gas. Occasionally the surface pattern indicates underlying structures.

FAULTS mark movement along breaks in the earth's crust. Oil may seep to the surface or accumulate along or against them.

OIL is, in its natural state, a complex mixture of various hydrocarbons (combinations of carbon and hydrogen). Of marine origin, oil is probably the product of the decomposition of innumerable microscopic animals deposited with sand and mud at the bottom of the sea.

The earth movements illustrated above explain the formation of 'traps' in which oil accumulates, but it must be understood that such movements, particularly the faults, could, on the contrary, have allowed the oil to escape.

Oils, indeed, being all more or less volatile, tend to work their way upwards. They may also seep into other rocks, evaporate in the atmosphere, or become oxidized in contact with aerated water. It would be a mistake to think of an oil-field as a subterranean lake. Petroleum, a more or less viscid liquid, soaks the rocks it encounters in its migrations. The expressive term 'reservoir rocks' aptly describes these strata, in which the pores of the rock or the spaces be-

paraffin base   asphalt base

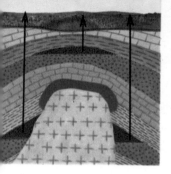

SALT DOMES, pushing up through Gulf Coast sediments and deforming them, make suitable structures to trap oil.

UNCONFORMITIES Oil may be confined where tilted layers have been worn down and later horizontal layers deposited on them.

tween the grains of sand become saturated with mineral oil. To locate oil traps a thorough geological and geophysical survey is undertaken, so as to discover the lie of the strata (with their anticlines, faults etc.) and thus be in a position to choose the best place in which to bore.

World production of petroleum is about 600 million tons a year.

BITUMENS AND ASPHALTS are the forms taken by hydrocarbons that have been more or less solidified by oxidation. Their presence indicates that an oil-field may exist.

OIL-SHALES are consolidated argillaceous shales consisting of solid hydrocarbons. They may be grey, brown or black, and there are vast layers of them in the world. Petrol may be obtained from them by distillation, but not cheaply enough to enable it to compete with the ordinary petrol marketed.

Oil shale with
fossil fish

Oil shale

OIL SHALE contains solid hydrocarbons mixed with plant remains. Oil shale has been mined and used for some time in Scotland. Should our richer deposits become depleted, we have well over 100 milliard barrels of oil locked up in oil shales. During World War II an experimental plant successfully made oil from oil shale. A ton of average oil shale, upon heating, yields about 25 gallons of petroleum, nearly 10,000 cubic feet of natural gas and ammonium compounds.

It is certain that folding and other crustal movements produced most of the traps in which oil accumulated. The oil and gas apparently migrated from a source rock through the porous sands until it was trapped against an impervious surface and slowly accumulated. Without these crustal traps petroleum may remain distributed in shales and sands, too diffuse to be produced economically at present prices. Oil shales and also oil sands contain huge reserves of solid hydrocarbons, from which oil can be made. How they will be utilized is, at the present moment, still an open question.

NATURAL GAS is found with petroleum, though some oil fields have very little gas and some gas fields yield no commercial oil. Chemically, natural gas is a mixture of the lighter chemicals found in petroleum—mainly methane with butane, propane, and other gases. Carbon dioxide, nitrogen, hydrogen sulphide and even helium may be present also.

The production of natural gas is widespread throughout North America, South America, Europe, Asia and Africa. Gas wells are usually situated some distance from the gas consumers, and in many places steel pipelines up to 1000 miles in length deliver the gas to the major industrial and distribution centres. If the natural pressure of the gas is

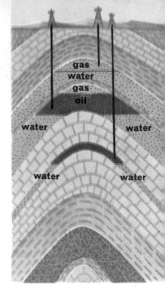

WELL FIELD producing gas from the upper zone, oil and gas from the middle zone, and oil below.

insufficient, pumping stations may be employed, while dehydrating plants are also common where low winter temperatures could cause crystals to form and block the pipes. Since the gas is odourless a substance having a distinctive smell may be added to simplify the discovery of leaks. Some gas is liquified and bottled; some is compressed for the extraction of natural petroleum. Over 75 per cent of natural gas goes for industrial uses.

In former times natural gas pressure on a pool of oil was frequently allowed to cause a "gusher". When this happened, a jet of oil was shot several hundred feet into the air and wasted.

RESIDUAL SOILS are those formed in place by the gradual decay of parent material. When cut through they show a gradual transition from fresh rock up to decayed rock to subsoil and topsoil. Residual soils usually form slowly. The deepening soil layer protects the rock beneath from further chemical action. Types of residual soils depend on the rock from which they form, climate, and other factors.

SOIL is the best known, most complex rock and, fortunately, one which has been studied a long time. The physical and chemical weathering of surface rock (parent material) with the addition of organic material, forms soil. Plants and animals (especially microscopic forms) contribute greatly to soil formation, as do climate, vegetation, time, slope, and drainage. The result of centuries of activity is a soil mantle from a few inches to a hundred feet thick, though the average depth of soil is only a foot or so. Since most life depends on soils, they should be preserved and skilfully managed.

TROPICAL RED SOILS are well-developed, well-drained soils resulting from the deep leaching action of much rain and the chemical action of warm air. These may be residual soils of great thickness. The leaching and oxidation make poor soil which may be exhausted after a few years of cultivation.

TRANSPORTED SOILS are developed on parent material that has been moved by wind, water, or ice. Huge deposits of wind-blown silt serve as the parent material for loess soils.

Soils may be classified in a half dozen ways, according to various properties. They may be classified on the basis of texture (size of particle), as clayey, silty, or sandy. Other classifications have been based on colour, parent material, type of crop raised, and many other bases. Most modern classifications begin with three great divisions or zones ranging from immature to mature soils. Three examples of well-developed soils are (1) the tropical red soils (true and modified laterites), (2) the northern forest soils (podsols) and their modifications, and (3) the grassland soils (chernozem and prairie soils).

NORTHERN FOREST SOILS illustrate different conditions from those above. These grey soils form under beds of spruce, pine, and fir needles which are acid in composition and decay slowly. The organic and inorganic materials mix poorly. Many of these soils of cooler regions have not been altered enough to make them good producers without special handling.

RED CLAY

GREY CLAY

CLAY was used by primitive men to make pottery not long after they first began to use stones as tools and weapons. After centuries of service, clay is still essential in many industries. About 35 million tons are mined annually and are used in bricks, pottery, chinaware, ceramic pipe, drilling muds, and for many other purposes. Clay minerals are complex aluminium silicates, often combined with water. Clay particles are small—less than 0.0001 inch. They stick together but are slippery when moist. Clays may come from granitic rocks, as a weathering product of the feldspars. They also form from weathered shales which came mainly from clay minerals originally. Clay deposits form on lake bottoms and in other quiet water, sometimes with annual layers (varves). One of the clay minerals is kaolin (p. 49).

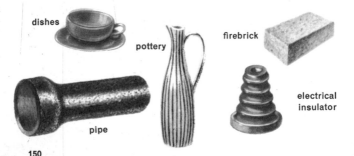

dishes

pottery

firebrick

pipe

electrical insulator

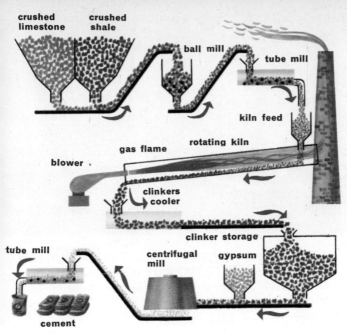

PORTLAND CEMENT is the best-known ingredient of artificial stone. It has largely replaced the older natural cement or hydraulic limestone. When limestone containing silica and clay was burned, the lime that formed would set under water, hence the name hydraulic lime.

Now, limestone and shale are crushed, dried, mixed in the correct proportions, and ground to a fine powder. The powdered mixture is burned in a sloping rotary kiln at about 2700 °F to form a glassy clinker. The clinker is crushed, a small amount of gypsum is added, and the mixture is reground to form cement. Over 200 million barrels of Portland cement are produced each year. Cement is mixed with sand, crushed rock, and water to make concrete.

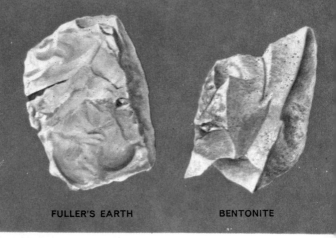

FULLER'S EARTH   BENTONITE

FULLER'S EARTH is clay or a silty clay material containing over half silica, valued for its decolourizing properties. Fuller's earth absorbs dark organic matter from fats, oils, and greases. First used to "full" or degrease woollen cloth, fuller's earth is used to bleach mineral and vegetable oils. It has the greasy feel of clay and usually breaks up in water. Colour varies from white to yellow, brown, and blue.

BENTONITE, first developed, like fuller's earth, for bleaching, has turned out to have even more important uses. It is used in soaps and washing compounds and is added to clays to increase their plasticity. Some bentonite, used as an aid in well drilling, expands and seals off water-bearing sands. Other varieties swell little when wet. Bentonite is also used for paper filler and in adhesives. It is a mixture of at least two aluminium and magnesium silicate minerals, and is usually regarded as weathered volcanic ash.

glacial sand

ocean beach sand

river sand and gravel

glacial sand (enlarged)   beach sand (enlarged)

SAND, GRAVEL, AND CRUSHED ROCK have about the lowest value per ton of any rock or mineral, yet all three are indispensable in modern construction. Sand in places is so plentiful that it shapes the landscape, giving beaches and deserts a quiet beauty of their own. Sand is a size term; although sand is usually composed largely of quartz, pure quartz sand (used in the manufacture of glass) is rare. On tropical shores, coral (lime) sands are common. Gypsum sands make up the snowy dunes in the White Sands National Monument. Other sands are rich in magnetite, monazite, garnet, ilmenite, and rutile. Some are mined as ores. But it is common quartz sand that helps make our concrete roads, bridges, and buildings.

Gravel, of glacial or stream origin, contains larger pebbles from a quarter of an inch up, cobbles, and even boulders, in a sand matrix. Washed, screened, and sorted, gravel is used for fill and in concrete. Limestone, basalt, and granite are crushed for road building, railway ballast, and concrete work.

BUILDING STONES are those cut to size for buildings or monuments. Ornamental stones are those used for finishing or decoration. Stone also has been used for sidewalks, curbing, and paving blocks. For building use, ease of quarrying, transportation, durability, colour,

RED GRANITE

GRANITE is famous for its beauty, strength, and durability —hence its wide use in monuments and buildings. It takes a high polish and is resistant to weathering. Its hardness and lack of bedding make quarrying difficult. Granites for building uses are classified by grain size— with preference for fine-grained rock.

COARSE GABBRO

BASALT is a name used by quarrymen for gabbro, diabase, or basalt. These hard, durable rocks are limited in building use because their iron minerals give a rusty stain as they weather. Basalt is excellent as crushed rock and is widely used. Other igneous rocks—rhyolites and felsites—are locally used as building stones.

"CRAB ORCHARD" STONE

SANDSTONE is relatively easy to quarry because it is bedded. Many sandstones are attractive and durable, and once were very fashionable in Eastern cities. Porous sandstone may not weather well and special treatment may be needed in cold regions. Otherwise, sandstones make attractive building stones. Colour and texture are variable.

weathering characteristics, and freedom from iron minerals are important. Of the building stones which are still widely used, the following general types are the best known. Many different kinds of marbles, limestones, and granites are used for varied effects.

LIMESTONE is widely used for public buildings, the most famous being the Portland Stone, from the Jurassic rocks of Dorset. This is white, even textured and durable. Many Jurassic oölitic limestones have also been used for building, e.g. Bath stone.

FOSSILIFEROUS LIMESTONE

MARBLE for building use also includes fine-grained ornamental limestones which are not true marbles. Marble is a classic stone, worked by sculptors as well as builders. Italian white and Belgian black marble are famous. Marbles may also be pink, yellow, and brown. They are softer and less resistant to weathering than granites.

BROWN MARBLE

SLATE is an unusual building stone used primarily in roofing and flooring, blackboards, and electrical switchboards. It breaks along cleavage planes in large flat sheets. Colour varies from black to green and red. Slate is durable and attractive as roofing and in floors and patios. Most British slate comes from North Wales, though some is quarried in Cornwall, the Lake District and Scotland.

GREY SLATE   RED SLATE

MORE INFORMATION

The following books will help you further with your studies, and tell you localities to search for specimens.

Read, H. H. RUTLEY'S MINERALOGY, Thos. Murby, London. A standard students' textbook with descriptions of all common minerals.

Holmes, A. PRINCIPLES OF PHYSICAL GEOLOGY, Nelson, London. An introductory textbook of theoretical geology.

Ford, W. DANA'S TEXTBOOK OF MINERALOGY, John Wiley, New York. A very complete advanced textbook.

The geology of the British Isles is summarized in a series BRITISH REGIONAL GEOLOGY, published by the Geological Survey. These handbooks give full references to more detailed sources of local information.

MUSEUMS AND EXHIBITS will show you more kinds of rocks and minerals than you will find on field trips. Use one to supplement the other. Some of the Museums with larger exhibits are listed below.

> **LONDON** Geological Museum, Exhibition Road, S.W.7. A general geological museum, but including galleries of Economic minerals and a notable collection of gemstones.
> British Museum (Natural History), Cromwell Road, S.W.7. A large and extensive exhibit of minerals and fossils.
> **BIRMINGHAM:** City Museum, Congreve Street.
> Bristol: City Museum, Queen's Road, Bristol 8.
> Cambridge: Sedgwick Museum of Geology, Downing Street.
> Cardiff: National Museum of Wales, Cathays Park.
> Edinburgh: Royal Scottish Museum, Chambers Street, Edinburgh 1.
> Glasgow: City Museum, Kelvingrove.
> Leeds: City Museum, Park Row, Leeds 1.
> Leicester: Museum and Art Gallery, The New Walk.
> Liverpool: City Museum, William Brown Street.
> Manchester: The Manchester Museum, University, Oxford Road.
> Newcastle upon Tyne: Hancock Museum, Barras Bridge.
> Nottingham: Natural History Museum, Wollaton Hall.
> Oxford: University Museum, Parks Road.
> Sheffield: City Museum, Weston Park, Sheffield 10.
> York: The Yorkshire Museum, Museum Street.

In addition to the above, many smaller museums contain geological collections, and most Universities and colleges have exhibits which may be viewed by appointment. Full details for British readers may be found in 'Museums and Galleries in Great Britain and Ireland', published annually by Index Publishers Ltd., 69 Victoria Street, S.W.1

INDEX

Asterisks (*) indicate illustrations.